Les Liaisons Dangereuses

Christopher Hampton was born in the Azores in 1946. He wrote his first play, *When Did You Last See My Mother?*, at the age of eighteen. Since then, his plays have included *The Philanthropist, Savages, Tales from Hollywood, Les Liaisons Dangereuses, White Chameleon, The Talking Cure, Embers, Appomattox, A German Life, Visit from an Unknown Woman* and *Atonement*. He has translated plays by Ibsen, Molière, Horváth, Chekhov, Florian Zeller (including *The Father* and *The Truth*) and Yasmina Reza (including *'Art', Life × 3* and *The God of Carnage*). His television work includes adaptations of *The History Man, Hotel du Lac* and *The Singapore Grip*. His screenplays include *The Honorary Consul, The Good Father, Dangerous Liaisons, Mary Reilly, Total Eclipse, The Quiet American, Atonement, Chéri, A Dangerous Method, The Father, The Son, Carrington, The Secret Agent* and *Imagining Argentina*, the last three of which he also directed.

also by Christopher Hampton

CHRISTOPHER HAMPTON: PLAYS ONE
(*The Philanthropist, Total Eclipse, Savages, Treats*)
CHRISTOPHER HAMPTON: PLAYS TWO
(*Tales from Hollywood, Les Liaisons Dangereuses,*
White Chameleon, The Talking Cure)
APPOMATTOX
EMBERS
A GERMAN LIFE
VISIT FROM AN UNKNOWN WOMAN
ATONEMENT

screenplays
COLLECTED SCREENPLAYS
(*Dangerous Liaisons, Carrington, Mary Reilly,*
A Bright Shining Lie, The Custom of the Country)
TOTAL ECLIPSE
THE SECRET AGENT & NOSTROMO

musicals
SUNSET BOULEVARD
STEPHEN WARD

translations
Yasmina Reza's
'ART'
THE UNEXPECTED MAN
CONVERSATIONS AFTER A BURIAL
LIFE X 3
THE GOD OF CARNAGE
Ibsen's
AN ENEMY OF THE PEOPLE
Chekhov's
THE SEAGULL
UNCLE VANYA
Ödön von Horváth's
TALES FROM THE VIENNA WOODS
FAITH, HOPE AND CHARITY
JUDGMENT DAY
Florian Zeller's
THE MOTHER *and* THE FATHER
THE TRUTH
THE LIE
HEIGHT OF THE STORM
THE SON

also available
HAMPTON ON HAMPTON
edited by Alistair Owen

CHRISTOPHER HAMPTON

Les Liaisons Dangereuses

from the novel by

CHODERLOS DE LACLOS

faber

First published in 1985
by Faber and Faber Limited
The Bindery, 51 Hatton Garden
London, ECIN 8HN

This revised edition published 2026

Typeset by Brighton Gray
Printed and bound in the UK by CPI Group (Ltd), Croydon CRO 4YY

A CIP record for this book
is available from the British Library

ISBN 978-0-571-40409-4

Printed and bound in the UK on FSC® certified paper in line with our continuing
commitment to ethical business practices, sustainability and the environment.
For further information see faber.co.uk/environmental-policy

Our authorised representative in the EU for product safety is
Easy Access System Europe, Mustamäe tee 50, 10621 Tallinn, Estonia
gpsr.requests@easproject.com

2 4 6 8 10 9 7 5 3

Introduction

It was the custom at the boarding school I attended, Lancing College, to allow one to practise a sport during the long weekday afternoons. I would regularly put myself down for a solitary cross-country run, jog to the bus stop, take a bus into Brighton and go to the cinema. There was a fleapit called the Continentale, which often showed risqué foreign films and was happy to admit a small fourteen-year-old, even to what were then known as X-films. So it was that I was able to see, in 1960, a film with a scandalous reputation, Roger Vadim's *Les Liaisons Dangereuses*. The film had been given a contemporary gloss, much of it set on ski slopes and in Paris cafés; I remember very little of it. Annette Stroyberg (who replaced Brigitte Bardot as Vadim's wife) played someone who seemed to be a combination of all the subsidiary female characters from the novel and was seen at one point with a telephone perched on her bottom. What I most remember is that the film starred two palpably great actors previously unknown to me: Gérard Philipe and Jeanne Moreau. I returned on the bus to Lancing stirred, but not particularly shaken.

* * *

I first read *Les Liaisons Dangereuses* when I was nineteen. First-year students of French Literature at my Oxford college were given various representative texts, one from each century, in order to choose in which period of literature they wanted to specialise. *Liaisons* (written in 1782) was the example from what Oxford designated the modern period. It seemed to me completely astonishing; and perhaps the most psychologically acute novel I'd ever read.

The book stayed with me, indelibly. Over the next decade I began to devise a way I might adapt it for the stage. When the brand-new National Theatre opened in 1976 and playwrights were invited to suggest ideas, I put forward the notion. Six weeks or so passed, no doubt during which people might have a chance to read what was, at the time, a relatively obscure foreign novel; after which I was summoned to the Literary Department to be told they really didn't think it was a very good idea, since, after all, it being an epistolary novel, the two main characters never even met. I tried to explain I had a plan to deal with this difficulty, but they were not to be swayed. Instead, very fortunately for me as it turned out, they proposed I translate a play called *Tales from the Vienna Woods* by a fascinating Austro-Hungarian dramatist, Ödön von Horváth, unperformed in English since his premature death in 1938.

Seven or eight years went by and I repeated my notion to a number of theatres and producers, always receiving the same dusty response. So when, in 1984, I was invited by the Royal Shakespeare Company to write a play of some scale for their London space, the Barbican, I decided to go ahead with the play I had in mind, without revealing its subject in advance except to its intended director, Howard Davies, who very much liked the idea and undertook to keep his mouth shut.

I handed in the play which, after the years of planning, I'd written relatively quickly, in about seven weeks – and it was received with an undeniable air of disappointment. This was not for the Barbican, was the unanimous verdict – and it was eventually given the end-of-season slot, twenty-three performances at The Other Place in Stratford, then a modest 150-seat shed with a corrugated tin roof at the far end of the car park. This was the first of the many strokes of luck which befell the play: its first audiences felt they were eavesdropping more or less illicitly on a series of private scandals, suspending them between complicity and horrified disapproval. This uncomfortable intimacy can only have contributed towards an almost unanimous critical acclaim, which caught the RSC almost entirely by surprise.

I had the sense something unusual was happening when I arrived to watch a Tuesday matinee in November. Before noon, standing outside among flurries of snow, a queue for returns stretched the length of the car park and round the corner into the street. Nevertheless, the RSC contained its excitement and confined itself to scheduling another twenty-two performances at the slightly larger Pit, the studio theatre at the Barbican. The remarkable cast, headed by Alan Rickman and Lindsay Duncan and including Juliet Stevenson and Fiona Shaw, with Lesley Manville in the role of the teenaged Cécile de Volanges, stayed intact for the moment and the tickets for the entire run disappeared in a matter of hours.

There was a strong case for extending the run in some way, but the RSC was not disposed to support this. They had had a great success the previous year with *La Dame aux Camélias*, but when transferred to the West End, it lost money. There wasn't really a broad public for these French things, was their considered opinion. A delightful couple of producers from Chicago, Frank and Woji Gero, had fallen in love with the play and proposed partnering with the RSC, but the RSC was not tempted. It seemed as if forty-five performances was the play's limit and that would be the end of it: not bad for a dramatisation of a little-known eighteenth-century French novel.

But Frank and Woji couldn't accept this. They offered to buy the play outright – and the RSC, retaining 2% of the profits and a few approval rights, sold it to them for £100,000. The Geros moved the play to the Ambassadors Theatre, where it ran for over 1,800 performances – the best part of five years.

The Ambassadors is one of the smallest theatres in the West End – three times as many seats as The Other Place, but still able to convey the illusion of intimacy. When it came to move *Liaisons* to Broadway, the belief, still held by many, that this was a work requiring an intimate space was thrown into question. One of my most vivid memories was finding Alan

Rickman in tears in his dressing room after the first preview at the 1,000-seat Music Box Theatre: he'd been performing the play for almost a year in Stratford and London and he felt the task of projecting it into an enormous theatre was an impossible one. But within a few performances his despair turned to exhilaration; and when the twenty weeks permitted at that time to a British company by American Equity was up, I had the pleasure of hearing him berate the American producers for their timidity in not continuing with American actors. There are so few plays these days, Alan was saying, that can effortlessly fill a big theatre. And I thought, after all, it was written for the Barbican.

* * *

Since then, *Liaisons* has proliferated unimaginably. There was the film, of course – indeed, there were two films, since Miloš Forman, with his version, *Valmont*, swung into direct competition with our *Dangerous Liaisons*. Since then, there's been a Korean film, a Chinese film, a French TV series and two separate TV series proposing prequels to the story (one with Lesley Manville) – not to mention the celebrated film cover version *Cruel Intentions*, an opera, a ballet and two new recent dramatisations, one French and one Australian. This list, I'm sure, is not exhaustive.

What is it about this extraordinary masterpiece that speaks so directly to us today? A distinguishing feature of masterpieces is that they appear to shift emphasis from one generation to another, remaining perpetually relevant. What in the 1980s seemed to be about the so-called 'me generation', about institutionalised selfishness and refusal to acknowledge any responsibility, has today shifted in focus to take in the repulsive concept of 'post-truth', where the most brazen lies are endlessly repeated until they're believed; where the boundless greed and appetite for exploitation exhibited by the international super-rich is indulged until it seems absolutely normal; and where individuals can be cancelled for reasons justifiable or unjustifiable until the implacable gods of the internet appear to be sated. By describing the underbelly of the aristocracy of pre-revolutionary France so truthfully, Laclos struck a chord that, as he hoped, has resounded down the centuries. We hear it and recognise it because it is all around us.

C.H.
March 2026

A Note on Laclos

In many respects, Pierre-Ambroise-François Choderlos de Laclos (1741–1803) is the perfect author: he wrote, at around the age of forty, one piece of fiction, which was not merely a masterpiece, but the supreme example of its genre, the epistolary novel; and then troubled the public no further.

Fortunately the obscurity from which, during his lifetime, this astonishing *tour de force* delivered him only briefly, has remained sufficiently deep to preserve his enigma. But those few facts which are known about him combine to throw an intriguing light on his rigorously classical novel.

A career soldier in an unusually extended period of peace, Laclos volunteered to serve in the American War of Independence, but lacked the means necessary to a campaign officer at the time. Instead, he was posted to a drab island in the Bay of Biscay and put in charge of its fortification. It was from here, bored and disappointed, that he wrote, famously, to a friend, announcing his intention to write something 'out of the ordinary, eye-catching, something that would resound around the world even after I had left it'. Few artists can have fulfilled their predictions so satisfactorily.

The novel caused an immediate and continuing sensation, and in its wake Laclos addressed himself to two other pieces of work: a treatise on women's education, unpublished in his lifetime; and a blistering demolition of one of France's military sacred cows, the tactician Maréchal de Vauban, which caused such offence that he was immediately rewarded with a series of particularly dreary provincial postings.

In the Revolution he was a Jacobin, not prominent but assiduous, a friend of Danton and the associate and secretary of the Duc d'Orléans, the king's liberal cousin, known as Philippe-Égalité. Inevitably during the Terror he was jailed twice and escaped execution, which he clearly expected, only narrowly and for reasons which have remained obscure. It took some time for him to be accepted back into the army, but eventually at the turn of the century he was made a general by Napoleon. The result, however, of this final success was that only a few weeks after arriving in Taranto in Southern Italy to take up a new command, he died of dysentery and malaria. His last letter was a dignified but urgent appeal to Napoleon, asking for support for his wife and three children.

Geometrician, inventor, military strategist, feminist, revolutionary, devoted husband and father: all of these qualities, some initially surprising in the author of *Les Liaisons dangereuses*, others less so, make their contribution towards a way of looking at this extraordinary and meteoric work; without, however, exhausting the pleasures of its rare mystery and merciless intelligence.

C.H.

Les Liaisons Dangereuses opened at The Other Place,
Stratford-upon-Avon, on 24 September 1985. The cast was
as follows:

La Marquise de Merteuil Lindsay Duncan
Mme de Volanges Fiona Shaw
Cécile Volanges Lesley Manville
Le Vicomte de Valmont Alan Rickman
Azolan Christopher Wright
Mme de Rosemonde Margery Mason
La Présidente de Tourvel Juliet Stevenson
Émilie Mary Jo Randle
Le Chevalier Danceny Sean Baker

Director Howard Davies
Designer Bob Crowley

It was subsequently produced at the Barbican London
in January 1986. It was then presented on Broadway at
the Music Box Theatre in April 1987 produced by James
M Nederlander the Schubert Organisation Inc Jerome
Minskoff Elizabeth I. McCann and Stephen Graham in
association with Jonathan Farkas.

Les Liaisons Dangereuses in this revised version opened in the Lyttelton auditorium of the National Theatre, London, on 1 April 2026. The cast, in order of speaking, was as follows:

Marquise de Merteuil Lesley Manville
Cécile de Volanges Hannah van der Westhuysen
Madame de Volanges Cat Simmons
Majordomo Ali Goldsmith
Vicomte de Valmont Aidan Turner
Azolan Sharif Afifi
Madame de Rosemonde Gabrielle Drake
Madame de Tourvel Monica Barbaro
Émilie Lucia Chocarro
Chevalier Danceny Darragh Hand
Adele Amy Macken
Father Anselme Curtis Angus
Julie Nandi Bhebhe
Society Dancers, Maids and Footmen Ishmail Aaron, Sharif Afifi, Curtis Angus, Charlotte Avery, Nandi Bhebhe, Lucia Chocarro, Liz Ewing, Ali Goldsmith, Georges Hann, Dianté Lodge, Amy Macken, Aisha Naamani, Bryony Pennington

UNDERSTUDIES
Marquise de Merteuil Charlotte Avery
Cécile de Volanges Amy Macken
Madame de Volanges/Madame de Rosemonde Liz Ewing
Majordomo/Azolan/Chevalier Danceny Ishmail Aaron
Vicomte de Valmont Sharif Afifi
Madame de Tourvel Nandi Bhebhe

Émilie Bryony Pennington
Offstage Swings Spike King and Katie Lusby

Recorded music performed by the Tippett Quartet and Shards

Director Marianne Elliott
Set Designer Rosanna Vize
Costume Designer Natalie Roar
Choreographer Tom Jackson Greaves
Composer Jasmin Kent Rodgman
Lighting Designer James Farncombe
Sound Designer Ian Dickinson for Autograph
Intimacy Director Ingrid Mackinnon
Fight Director   Sam Lyon-Behan
Casting Alastair Coomer CDG and Naomi Downham
Voice and Dialect Coach Hazel Holder
Associate Director Mumba Dodwell
Associate Wigs, Hair and Make-up Designer Adele Brandman
Assistant Voice Coach Zoe Littleton

Characters

La Marquise de Merteuil

Madame de Volanges

Cécile Volanges

Le Vicomte de Valmont

Azolan

Madame de Rosemonde

Madame de Tourvel

Émilie

Le Chevalier Danceny

**Various Servants
in the Merteuil, Rosemonde,
Tourvel and Valmont households**

The action takes place in various salons
and bedrooms in a number of hôtels
and châteaux in and around Paris,
and in the Bois de Vincennes,
one autumn and winter in the 1780s

LES LIAISONS DANGEREUSES

To Roger

Comme devant tant d'oeuvres de notre temps –
pas seulement littéraires – le lecteur des *Liaisons*
eût pu dire: 'Ça ne peut pas durer ainsi.'

André Malraux, 1969

Act One

ONE

A warm evening in August. The principal salon in the Paris hôtel of Mme la Marquise de Merteuil. A lavish ball is in progress. Suggestions of great opulence. In due course, the Marquise de Merteuil herself, a respectable widow of considerable means, detaches herself from the dance, bringing with her a slim and attractive blonde girl, Cécile de Volanges. Mme de Volanges, Cécile's mother and Merteuil's cousin, herself a widow, follows the two of them, bustling along in their wake.

Merteuil So, my dear, you've left the convent for good?

Cécile Yes, Madame.

Merteuil And how are you adapting to the outside world?

Cécile Very well, I think. I'm so excited to have my own bedroom and dressing room.

Volanges I've advised her to watch and learn and be quiet except when spoken to. She's very naturally still prone to confusion.

Merteuil Never mind, my dear, you'll soon get used to us. We must see what we can devise for your amusement.

Merteuil's Majordomo appears, advances unhurriedly across the room and murmurs something in Merteuil's ear. Merteuil sighs.

He's very late. You'd better show him up.

The Majordomo bows and withdraws. Merteuil turns back to the others.

Valmont is here.

Volanges You receive him, do you?

Merteuil Yes. So do you.

Volanges I thought perhaps that under the circumstances . . .

Merteuil Under what circumstances? I don't believe I have any grounds for self-reproach . . .

Volanges On the contrary. As far as I know, you're virtually unique in that respect.

Merteuil . . . and, of course, if I had, he would no longer be calling on me.

Cécile has been following this exchange closely, frowning in the attempt to make sense of it. Now Mme de Volanges turns to her.

Volanges Monsieur le Vicomte de Valmont, my child, whom you very probably don't remember, except that he is conspicuously charming, never opens his mouth without first calculating what damage he can do.

Cécile Then why do you receive him, Maman?

Volanges Everyone receives him. He has a distinguished name, a large fortune and a very pleasant manner. You'll soon find that society is riddled with such inconsistencies: we're all aware of them, we all deplore them and in the end we all accommodate to them. Besides which, people are quite rightly afraid to provoke his malice. No one has the slightest respect for him; but everyone is very nice to him.

She breaks off as the Majordomo reappears, escorting Le Vicomte de Valmont, a strikingly elegant figure. Valmont crosses the room and bows formally to Merteuil in a gesture which also takes in the others.

Valmont Madame.

Merteuil Vicomte.

Volanges What a pleasant surprise.

Valmont How delightful to see you, Madame.

Volanges You remember my daughter, Cécile.

Valmont Well, indeed, but who could have foretold she would flower so gracefully?

Volanges is not best pleased by this remark; Valmont turns his attention back to Merteuil.

I wanted to call on you before leaving the city.

Merteuil Oh, I'm not sure we can allow that. Why should you want to leave?

Valmont Paris in August, you know: and it's time I paid a visit on my old aunt, I've neglected her disgracefully.

Merteuil I approve of your aunt. She takes such an intelligent interest in the young, she's been able to maintain a kind of youthfulness of her own. All the same . . .

Volanges Will you please give Madame de Rosemonde our warmest regards? She's been good enough to invite us to stay at the château, and I hope perhaps later in the season . . .

Valmont I shall make a point of it, Madame.

Volanges turns to Cécile, registering her interest in Valmont.

Volanges I think it may be time we took you home.

Cécile I had to be in bed by nine at the convent.

Valmont So I should hope.

The ladies have risen to their feet by now, and Merteuil signals to a Footman, who moves over to escort Mme de Volanges and Cécile from the room, amid general salutations. Valmont has bowed to them and now waits,

*in a more private corner of the room. When Merteuil
moves back towards him, it's as if they're alone together.
They look at each other for a while before Merteuil
speaks, in a quite different tone.*

Merteuil Your aunt?

Valmont That's right.

Merteuil Whatever for? I thought she'd already made
arrangements to leave you all her money.

Valmont She has. But there are other considerations, family
obligations, that kind of thing.

Merteuil Do you know why I summoned you here this
evening?

Valmont I'd hoped it might be for the pleasure of my
company.

Merteuil I need you to carry out a heroic enterprise.
Something for your memoirs.

Valmont I don't know when I shall ever find the time to
write my memoirs.

Merteuil Then I'll write them.

Silence. Valmont smiles at her.

You remember when Gercourt left me?

Valmont Yes.

Merteuil And went off with that fat mistress of yours,
whose name escapes me?

Valmont Yes, yes.

Merteuil No one has ever done that to me before. Or to
you, I imagine.

Valmont I was quite relieved to be rid of her, frankly.

Merteuil No, you weren't.

Silence.

One of Gercourt's more crass and boring topics of conversation was what exactly he would look for in a wife, what qualities, when the moment came for him, as he put it, to settle down.

Valmont Yes.

Merteuil He has a ludicrous theory that blondes are inherently more modest and respectable than any other species of girl and he's also unshakeably prejudiced in favour of convent education. And now he's found the ideal candidate.

Valmont Cécile Volanges?

Merteuil Very good.

Valmont And her sixty thousand a year, that must have played some part in his calculations.

Merteuil I tell you, if she were an uncloistered brunette, she could be worth twice that, and he wouldn't go near her. His priority, you see, is a guaranteed virtue.

Valmont I wonder if I'm beginning to guess what it is you're intending to propose.

Merteuil Gercourt is with his regiment in Corsica until October. That should give you plenty of time.

Valmont You mean to . . . ?

Merteuil She's a rosebud.

Valmont You think so?

Merteuil And he'd get back from honeymoon to find himself the laughing stock of Paris.

Valmont Well . . .

Merteuil Yes. Love and revenge: two of your favourites.

Silence. Valmont considers for a moment. Finally, he shakes his head, smiling.

Valmont No, I can't.

Merteuil What?

Valmont You know how difficult I find it to disobey your orders. But really, I can't.

Merteuil Why not?

Valmont It's too easy. It is. What is she, sixteen, she's seen nothing, she knows nothing, she's bound to be curious, she'd be on her back before you'd unwrapped the first bunch of flowers. Any one of a dozen men could manage it. I have my reputation to think of.

Merteuil I think you underestimate her. She's very pretty, and she has a rather promising air of sensuality.

Valmont I hadn't noticed.

Merteuil There is someone who's already fallen for her: young Danceny. He goes round to sing duets with her.

Valmont And you think he'd like to try a little close harmony?

Merteuil Yes, but he's as timid and inexperienced as she is, we couldn't rely on him. So, you see, it'll just have to be you.

Valmont I hate to disappoint you.

Merteuil I think you really are going to refuse me. Aren't you?

Silence. Valmont looks at her.

Valmont I can see I'm going to have to tell you everything.

Merteuil Of course you are.

Valmont Yes. Well. My trip to the country to visit my more or less immortal aunt. The fact of the matter is that it's the first step towards the most ambitious plan I've ever undertaken.

Merteuil Well, go on.

Valmont You see, my aunt is not on her own just at the moment. She has a young friend staying with her. Madame de Tourvel.

Merteuil Yes.

Valmont She is my plan.

Merteuil You can't mean it.

Valmont Why not? To seduce a woman famous for strict morals, religious fervour and the happiness of her marriage: what could possibly be more prestigious?

Merteuil I think there's something degrading about having a husband for a rival. It's humiliating if you fail and commonplace if you succeed. Where is he, anyway?

Valmont He's presiding over some labyrinthine case in Burgundy, which I'm reliably informed will drag on for months.

Merteuil I can't believe this. Apart from anything else, she's such a frump. Bodice up to her ears in case you might catch a glimpse of a square inch of flesh . . .

Valmont You're right, clothes don't suit her.

Merteuil How old is she?

Valmont Twenty-two.

Merteuil And she's been married . . . ?

Valmont Two years.

Merteuil Even if you succeed, you know what?

Valmont What?

Merteuil All you'll get from her is what she gives her husband. I don't think you can hope for any actual pleasure. They never let themselves go, those people. If you ever make her heart beat faster, it won't be pleasure, it'll be fear. I sometimes wonder about you, Vicomte. How could you make such a fool of yourself over a complete nonentity?

Valmont Take care, now, you're speaking of the woman I . . .

Merteuil Yes?

Valmont I've set my heart on.

Silence. He smiles at her.

I haven't felt so strongly about anything since you and I were together.

Merteuil And you're going to pass up this wonderful opportunity for revenge?

Valmont If I have to.

Merteuil You don't have to. I won't tell anyone about this bizarre aberration of yours.

Valmont I think you'll have to wait at least until I've had her before I can allow you to insult her. And I can't agree with your theory about pleasure. You see, I have no intention of breaking down her prejudices. I want her to believe in God and virtue and the sanctity of marriage, and still not be able to stop herself. I want passion, in other words. Not the kind we're used to, which is as cold as it's superficial, I don't get much pleasure out of that any more. No. I want the excitement of watching her betray everything that's most important to her. Surely you understand that. I thought betrayal was your favourite word.

Merteuil No, no – cruelty. I always think that has a nobler ring to it.

Valmont You're terrible, you're a hundred times worse than I'll ever be; since we started this little mission, you've made many more converts than I have, you make me feel like an amateur.

Merteuil And so you are; really, you might just as well be in love.

Valmont Well, if love is not being able to think of anything else all day or dream of anyone else all night, perhaps I am: that's why I must have her, to rescue myself from this ridiculous position.

Merteuil Love is something you use, not something you fall into, like a quicksand, don't you remember? It's like medicine, you use it as a lubricant to nature.

They look at each other.

Valmont How is Belleroche?

Merteuil Well, he *is* in love. I thought it might be time to end it last week, I tried to pick a quarrel, but he looked so woebegone, I relented, and we spent the best night we've ever had. Since then, of course, he's been more assiduous than ever. But I'm keeping him at arm's length because I'm so pleased with him. He hasn't learned that excess is something you reserve for people you're about to leave.

Valmont So you're not about to leave him?

Merteuil No, I told you, at the moment I'm very pleased with him.

Valmont And he's currently your only lover?

Merteuil Yes.

Valmont I think you should take another. I think it most unhealthy, this exclusivity.

Merteuil You're not jealous, are you?

Valmont Well, of course I am. Belleroche is completely undeserving.

Merteuil I thought he was one of your closest friends.

Valmont Exactly, so I know what I'm talking about. No, I think you should organise an infidelity. With me, for example.

Merteuil You refuse to grant me a simple favour, and then you expect to be indulged?

Valmont It's only because it is so simple. It wouldn't feel like a conquest. I have to follow my destiny, you see. I have to be true to my profession.

Merteuil Well . . .

Long silence. They look at each other, Merteuil amused, Valmont eager.

In that case, come back when you've succeeded with Madame de Tourvel.

Valmont Yes?

Merteuil And I will offer you . . . a reward.

Valmont My love.

Merteuil But I shall require proof.

Valmont Certainly.

Merteuil Written proof.

Valmont Ah.

Merteuil Not negotiable.

Valmont rises to his feet and bows. Merteuil watches him, smiling.

Valmont And I'm sure you'll find someone to help you out with the little Volanges.

Merteuil She's so lovely. If my morals were less austere, I'd take it on myself.

Valmont You are an astonishing woman.

Merteuil Thank you.

Valmont I'm only sorry you haven't sufficient confidence in me to give me my reward in advance.

Merteuil Goodnight, Vicomte.

He kisses her hand, releases it and stands looking at her for a moment, before turning away.

TWO

Three weeks later. Early evening. The principal salon in Mme de Rosemonde's château in the country. The late sun slants through the French windows. Valmont is interviewing Azolan, his valet de chambre, *a dapper young man, resplendent in the livery of a* chasseur.

Valmont So he grasped what was going on, did he?

Azolan Oh, yes, sir. I was watching him and he was watching you.

Valmont I just hope he was better at understanding what was happening than he was at shadowing me; I sat down for a rest on the way and he was trampling about behind some bush, making so much noise I had a good mind to give him a legful of small shot. Except then I suppose he'd have had even more trouble keeping up.

Azolan He knew what you were doing: and after you'd gone he talked to the family.

Valmont I must say the family was very well chosen.

Azolan Thank you, sir.

Valmont Solidly respectable, gratifyingly tearful, no suspiciously pretty girls. Well done.

Azolan I do my best for you, sir.

Valmont And not even unduly expensive. Fifty-six livres to save an entire family from ruin, that seems a genuine bargain.

Azolan These days, my lord, you can find half a dozen like that, any village in the country.

Valmont Really? I must say, it's no longer a mystery to me why people fall so easily into the habit of charitable enterprises. All that humble gratitude. It was most affecting.

Azolan Certainly brought a tear to my eye, sir.

Valmont How are you getting on with the maid?

Azolan Julie? Tell you the truth, it's been a bit boring. If I wasn't so anxious to keep your lordship abreast, I think I'd only have bothered the once. I'm not sure she doesn't feel the same, but, you know, what else is there to do in the country?

Valmont Yes, it wasn't so much the details of your intimacy I was after, it was whether she's agreed to bring me Madame de Tourvel's letters, and do you think she'll keep her mouth shut?

Azolan She won't steal the letters, sir.

Valmont She won't?

Azolan As for keeping her mouth shut, I haven't asked her to keep her mouth shut, because that's the one thing most likely to give her the idea of opening it.

Valmont You may well be right. But look, Madame de Tourvel told me she'd been warned about me: that means some officious friend must have written to her about me. I need to know who.

Azolan I shouldn't worry about all that, if I was you, sir. If she's interested enough to have you followed, I'd say it was only a matter of time.

Valmont Do you think so?

Azolan Anyway, apparently she keeps her letters in her pockets.

Valmont I wish I knew how to pick pockets. Why don't our parents ever teach us anything useful?

Pause, as Valmont considers.

Where do you and Julie meet?

Azolan Oh, in my room, sir.

Valmont And is she coming tonight?

Azolan Afraid so.

Valmont Then I think I may have to burst in on you. See if blackmail will succeed better than bribery. About two o'clock suit you? I don't want to embarrass you, will that give you enough time?

Azolan Ample, sir.

Valmont Good.

Azolan Then you won't have to pay her, sir, will you?

Valmont Oh, I think if she delivers, we can afford to be generous, don't you?

Azolan It's your money, sir.

Valmont Don't worry, I shan't overlook your contribution.

Azolan Well, that's very decent of you, sir.

Valmont looks up at the sound of approaching female voices. He turns back to Azolan.

Valmont Off you go, then. See you at two.

Azolan Right, sir. I'll be sure to arrange her so she can't say she's there to borrow a clothes brush.

He leaves by one door as Mme de Rosemonde and Mme de Tourvel arrive by another. Mme de Rosemonde is eighty-four, arthritic but lively, intelligent and sympathetic; and Mme de Tourvel is a handsome woman of twenty-two, dressed not as Merteuil described, but in an elegantly plain linen gown. She is clearly in a state of considerable excitement.

Rosemonde Here he is. I said he would be here.

Valmont rises to greet them. Tourvel cannot help reacting to his presence.

Valmont Ladies.

Rosemonde Madame de Tourvel has some mystery to reveal to us.

Tourvel To you, Madame, to you.

Valmont Oh, well, then, perhaps I should go for a walk.

Tourvel No, no, it, it concerns you as well. I mean, it particularly concerns you. In fact, I must begin by asking you some questions.

Valmont Very well. Just let me help my aunt to her chair.

Rosemonde Thank you, my boy.

Valmont installs Mme de Rosemonde in her armchair, then turns his attention back to Mme de Tourvel.

Valmont Now.

Tourvel Where did you go this morning, Monsieur?

Valmont Well, as you know, I was up early to go out hunting.

Tourvel And did you succeed in making a kill this time?

Valmont No, I've had the most wretched luck ever since I arrived here. Also I'm a terrible shot.

Tourvel But on this occasion, Monsieur le Vicomte, what exactly was it you were hunting?

Valmont I'm sorry, I'm afraid I don't quite follow . . .

Tourvel You may as well own up, Monsieur, I know where you were this morning.

Rosemonde I think it's time somebody explained to me what's going on.

Tourvel Georges, my footman, just happened to be in the village earlier today . . .

Valmont I do hope you haven't been listening to servants' gossip.

Tourvel I can see Monsieur de Valmont is determined not to tell you, so I shall have to. There's a family in the village, the man has been ill, he found himself not able to pay his taxes this year. So this morning the bailiff arrived to seize their few sticks of furniture. Whereupon your nephew, whose valet had been making enquiries in the village to see if anyone was suffering from particular hardship, arrived, paid off the family's debts and added a generous contribution to help them back on their feet again.

Rosemonde Is this true, my dear?

Valmont Well, I . . . it's simply . . . Yes.

Mme de Rosemonde rises to her feet and spreads out her arms.

Rosemonde You dear boy, come and let me give you a hug!

Valmont crosses to her and they embrace. Then Valmont turns and advances towards Mme de Tourvel, smiling radiantly, his arms outstretched. A spasm of panic crosses her face but she has no choice but to submit to the embrace.

It's so like you to make a secret of something like that.

In the ensuing silence, Mme de Tourvel moves across to the tapestry frame, and picks up the already-threaded needle. But her hands are shaking so badly, she has to put it down again.

We must visit this family in the morning, my dear, to see if we can help in any other way.

Tourvel Yes, I'd like that.

Valmont Do sit down, Aunt.

Rosemonde No, I must try to find Monsieur le Curé. I shan't be long, but I do want to tell him about this before he leaves, he'll be so pleased.

She bustles out of the room, and a long silence ensues. Mme de Tourvel makes a renewed and determined effort to get to grips with her tapestry; Valmont finds a chair facing her, watches and waits. The light is beginning to die. Finally, Mme de Tourvel, struggling for composure, feels compelled to break the silence.

Tourvel I can't understand how someone whose instincts are so generous could lead such a dissolute life.

Valmont I'm afraid you have an exaggerated idea both of my generosity and of my depravity. If I knew who'd given you such a dire account of me, I might be able to defend myself; since I don't, let me make a confession: I'm afraid the key to the paradox lies in a certain weakness of character.

Tourvel I don't see how so thoughtful an act of charity could be described as weak.

Valmont I've spent my life surrounded by immoral people; I've allowed myself to be influenced by them and sometimes even taken pride in outshining them. Whereas, in this case, I've simply fallen under a quite opposite kind of influence: yours.

Tourvel You mean you wouldn't have done it . . . ?

Valmont Not without your example, no. It was by way of
an innocent tribute to your goodness.

> *There's a pause, during which Mme de Tourvel, uncertain
> how to react, abandons her tapestry, hovers indecisively
> for a second and then sits, perching on the edge of a
> chaise-longue.*

You see how weak I am? I promised myself I was never
going to tell you. It's just, looking at you . . .

Tourvel Monsieur.

Valmont You needn't worry, I have no illicit intentions,
I wouldn't dream of insulting you. But I do love you.
I adore you.

> *He's across the room in an instant, drops to one knee in
> front of her and takes her hands in his.*

Please help me!

> *Mme de Tourvel wrenches her hands free.*

Tourvel Will you leave me now?

> *Valmont rises and moves away across the room.*

Valmont I shouldn't have said anything, I know I shouldn't,
I'm sorry. But really, you have nothing to fear. Nothing at
all. Tell me what to do, show me how to behave, I'll do
anything you say.

Tourvel I thought the least I could hope for was that you
would respect me.

Valmont But I do, of course I do!

Tourvel Then forget all this, don't say another word,
you've offended me deeply, it's unforgivable.

Valmont I thought you might give me some credit for being
honest.

Tourvel On the contrary, this confirms everything I've been told about you. I'm beginning to think you may well have planned the whole exercise.

Valmont When I came to visit my aunt, I had no idea you were here: not that it would have disturbed me in the slightest if I had known. You see, up until then, I'd only ever experienced desire. Love, never.

Tourvel That's enough.

Valmont No, no, you made an accusation, you must allow me the opportunity to defend myself. Now, you were there when my aunt asked me to stay a little longer, and at that time I only agreed in deference to her, although I was already by no means unaware of your beauty.

Tourvel Monsieur . . .

Valmont No, the point is, all this has nothing to do with your beauty. As I got to know you, I began to realise that beauty is the least of your qualities. I became fascinated by your goodness, I was drawn in by it, I didn't understand what was happening to me, and it was only when I began to feel actual physical pain every time you left the room, that it finally dawned on me: I was in love, for the first time in my life. I knew it was hopeless, of course, but that didn't matter to me, because it wasn't like it always had been, it wasn't that I wanted to have you, no. All I wanted was to deserve you.

Mme de Tourvel rises decisively to her feet.

Tourvel I really will have to leave you, Monsieur, you seem determined to persist with a line of argument you must know I ought not to listen to and I don't want to hear.

Valmont No, no, please, sit down, sit down. I've already told you, I'll do anything you say.

Silence. They watch each other. Eventually, Mme de Tourvel sits down again.

Tourvel There's only one thing I would like you to do for me.

Valmont What? What is it?

Tourvel But I don't see how I can ask you, I'm not even sure if I want to put myself in the position of being beholden to you.

Valmont Oh, please, no, I insist, if you're good enough to give me an opportunity to do something you want, anything, it's I who will be beholden to you.

Mme de Tourvel looks as him for a moment with characteristic openness.

Tourvel Very well, then, I would like you to leave this house.

There flashes momentarily across Valmont's face the expression of a chess champion who has just lost his queen.

Valmont I don't see why that should be necessary.

Tourvel Let's just say you've spent your life making it necessary.

By now, Valmont has recovered his equilibrium; and thought very fast.

Valmont Well then, of course, whatever you say. I couldn't possibly refuse you.

It's Mme de Tourvel's turn to be surprised.

Will you allow me to give my aunt, say, twenty-four hours' notice?

Tourvel Well, yes, naturally.

Valmont I shall find something in my mail tomorrow morning which obliges me to return at once to Paris.

Tourvel Thank you, I'd be very grateful.

Valmont Perhaps I might be so bold as to ask a favour in return.

Mme de Tourvel frowns, hesitating.

I think it would only be just to let me know which of your friends has blackened my name.

Tourvel You know very well that's impossible, Monsieur. If friends of mine have warned me against you, they've done so purely in my own interest and I could hardly reward them with betrayal, could I? I must say, you devalue your generous offer if you want to use it as a bargaining point.

Valmont Very well, I withdraw the request. I hope you won't think I'm bargaining if I ask you to let me write to you.

Tourvel Well . . .

Valmont And hope that you will do me the kindness of answering my letters.

Tourvel I'm not sure a correspondence with you is something a woman of honour could permit herself.

Valmont I really don't see how you could possibly be harmed by conceding me this very minor but, as far as I'm concerned, vitally important consolation.

Tourvel I would welcome the chance to prove to you that what motivates me in this is not hatred or resentment, but . . .

Valmont But what?

But Mme de Tourvel seems unable to find a satisfactory answer to this. Valmont reaches for her hand.

Tourvel For God's sake, Monsieur, please, leave me alone!

Valmont I only want to say what I hardly thought it would be possible for me to say to you: goodbye.

He kisses her hand.

I'll write soon.

He hurries away into the darkness, just failing to muffle a discreet sob. Mme de Tourvel is left alone, rooted to the chaise-longue. She looks terrified.

THREE

Another ball: Merteuil, Cécile and Mme de Volanges are dancing. Every now and then, Merteuil and Cécile are briefly adjacent, at which point Merteuil seizes the opportunity to carry on a conversation, as is presently the case.

Merteuil So you're telling me that during your music lessons, Monsieur Danceny has been passing you letters?

Cécile Yes, Madame.

Merteuil I see.

They are separated from one another by the dance; eventually they come back together again.

Cécile Would it be very wrong of me to answer them?

Merteuil It most certainly would. Especially in the circumstances.

Cécile In what circumstances?

But Merteuil is swept away before she can answer; Cécile has to wait until they're once again next to one another.

Merteuil The fact is, my dear, your marriage has been arranged.

Cécile My marriage? To whom?

Merteuil A man I know slightly. Monsieur le Comte de Gercourt.

Cécile What's he like?

Merteuil Well . . .

Again, they're parted; when they come together the next time, Cécile doesn't hesitate.

Cécile How old is he?

Merteuil Thirty-six.

Cécile Thirty-six? He's an old man!

They're pulled apart again. When they come back together, Merteuil is ready.

Merteuil Maybe there is a way to let you write to Monsieur Danceny.

Cécile Oh, Madame!

Merteuil You would of course have to show me both sides of the correspondence.

Cécile I can't show you the letters I've already sent him . . .

She breaks off, aware she's given herself away; but Merteuil's smile, as the dance carries her off, is indulgent.

FOUR

A couple of days later. The middle of the night. A bedroom in a house on the outskirts of Paris which belongs to Émilie, a courtesan. She's in bed with Valmont, lying in his arms, her eyes flashing in the candlelight. He seems lost in thought. Émilie shifts her position and he smiles down at her.

Valmont I thought the Dutch were supposed to be famous for their capacity for alcohol.

Émilie Three bottles of burgundy and a bottle of cognac would finish anybody.

Valmont Did he drink that much?

Émilie You were pouring.

Valmont I hope you're not missing him.

Émilie Don't be silly. I just don't think it was necessary to bundle him into your carriage.

Valmont Man in that condition, I thought it best to send him back to his house.

Émilie This is his house.

Valmont Oh. I thought it was your house.

Émilie He owns it. I just live in it. And he's so rarely in France. Seems a shame.

She grins broadly.

Valmont I must say, Émilie, I do think it's the height of bad manners to talk about some foreigner when you're in bed with me. I think some appropriate punishment is called for. Turn over.

Émilie hesitates, looking up at him for a moment. Then she breaks into a smile.

Émilie All right.

She does so, looking up at him expectantly.

Valmont Now, do you have pen, ink and writing paper?

Émilie is puzzled. After a while, she answers.

Émilie Yes, over there, in the bureau. Why?

Instead of answering, Valmont gets out of bed, crosses the room, finds what he's looking for in the bureau and brings it back to the bed. He puts down the pen and inkwell carefully, twitches back the bedclothes, spreads a sheet of paper across the small of Émilie's back, arranges himself comfortably and reaches for the pen.

Valmont Now don't move.

Émilie is still puzzled. But she submits graciously enough. Valmont begins to write.

'My dear Madame de Tourvel . . . I have just come . . . to my desk . . .'

Émilie understands now. She turns her head to smile up at him.

Don't move, I said.

As he resumes writing, lights come up on the other side of the stage, where Mme de Tourvel walks through Mme de Rosemonde's garden, reading the letter.

'. . . in the middle of a stormy night, during which I have been tossed from exaltation to exhaustion and back again. The position in which I find myself as I write has made me more than ever aware of the power of love. I can scarcely control myself sufficiently to put my thoughts in order; but despite these torments I guarantee that at this moment I am far happier than you. I hope one day you may feel the kind of disturbance afflicting me now: meanwhile please excuse me while I take steps to calm what I can only describe as a mounting excitement.'

He moves aside paper, pen and inkwell and leans back to nuzzle Émilie, who hasn't moved.

We'll finish it later, will we?

The lights fade on Valmont and Émilie; and focus shifts to Mme de Tourvel, who is evidently extremely moved by what she's reading.

FIVE

Ten days later. A September afternoon. Valmont is taking tea with La Marquise de Merteuil in her grand salon.

Merteuil It sounds to me as if you made a serious tactical error. Shouldn't you have taken Madame de Tourvel there and then on the chaise-longue?

Valmont I was expecting my aunt and the curé to appear at any moment.

Merteuil Well, it would have been the most interesting thing to happen to them for years.

Valmont No, it wasn't at all the moment: I want her to surrender, but not before she's put up a fight.

Merteuil She seems to be: she's succeeded in getting rid of you altogether.

Valmont But I got her to agree to let me write to her.

Merteuil Well, in the unlikely event of her defences being pierced by your eloquence, you're not going to be there to take advantage of it, are you? And by the following day they'll be back in full repair.

Valmont Naturally, writing to someone is a poor substitute, but since I really had no choice in the matter, at least I've found a way to keep the thing alive.

Merteuil Perhaps.

Valmont I know you're incurably sceptical, but for me, with a woman, this is by far the best stage, it's what men talk about all the time but hardly ever experience, the real intoxication: when you know she loves you, but you're still not quite certain of victory.

Merteuil You know she loves you, then?

Valmont Oh, yes. I left my man there to keep an eye on things and a hand on the maid, who's been most cooperative since I caught them in bed together: and he tells me that when my first letter arrived, she took it to her room and sat turning it over for hours, sighing and weeping. So it seems a reasonable enough conclusion.

Merteuil says nothing, but her expression remains dubious.

And the maid helped us to another discovery which might interest you.

Merteuil Oh, yes?

Valmont Can you guess who it was who kept writing to my beauty, warning her to steer clear of the world's vilest pervert, namely me? Your damned cousin, the Volanges bitch.

Merteuil bursts out laughing.

It's all very well for you to laugh, she's set me back at least a month.

Merteuil It's not that.

Valmont She wanted me away from Madame de Tourvel: well, now I am, and I intend to make her suffer for it. Your plan to ruin her daughter: are you making any progress? Is there anything I can do to help? I'm entirely at your disposal.

Merteuil Well, as a matter of fact, my dear Vicomte, your presence here today forms part of my plan. I'm expecting Danceny at any moment and I want you to help me stiffen his resolve, if that's the phrase. And then I've arranged a little scene I hope you may find entertaining: yes, I'm sure you will.

Valmont Is that all you're going to say?

Merteuil Yes, I think so.

Valmont Has Danceny not been a great success?

Merteuil He's been disastrous. Like most intellectuals, he's intensely stupid. He really is a most incompetent boy. Charming, but hopeless.

Valmont You'd better bring me up to date.

Merteuil Well, I've become extremely thick with little Cécile. We go to my box at the Opéra and chatter away all evening. I'm really quite jealous of whoever's in store for her. She has a certain innate duplicity which is going to stand her in very good stead. She has no character and no morals, she's altogether delicious.

Valmont But what's happened?

Merteuil She and Danceny are head over heels in love; but all his energies go into writing her poems of great ingenuity and minimum impact. I went to considerable lengths to arrange a rendezvous between them, and after all that, what do I find? Danceny has managed to hold her hand for five seconds and, when asked to let go, to Cécile's extreme annoyance, he did. You really have to put some backbone into him. Afterwards the little one said to me, 'Oh, Madame, I wish you were Danceny': and, do you know, just for a minute, I wished I was.

Valmont I often wonder how you managed to invent yourself.

Merteuil I had no choice, did I? I'm a woman. Women are obliged to be far more skilful than men, because whoever wastes time cultivating inessential skills? You think you put as much ingenuity into winning us as we put into losing: well, it's debatable, I suppose, but from then on, you hold every ace in the pack. You can ruin us whenever the fancy takes you: all we can achieve by denouncing you is to enhance your prestige. We can't even get rid of you when we want to: we're compelled to unstitch, painstakingly,

what you would just cut through. We either have to devise
some way of making you want to leave us, so you'll feel
too guilty to harm us; or find a reliable means of blackmail:
otherwise you can destroy our reputation and our life with
a few well-chosen words. So of course I had to invent –
not only myself, but ways of escape no one else has ever
thought of, not even I, because I had to be fast enough on
my feet to know how to improvise. And I've succeeded,
because I always knew I was born to dominate your sex
and avenge my own.

Valmont Yes; but what I asked you was how.

Merteuil When I came out into society, I was Cécile's
age, I'd already realised that the role I was condemned
to, namely to keep quiet and do as I was told, gave me
the perfect opportunity to listen and pay attention: not to
what people told me, which was naturally of no interest,
but to whatever it was they were trying to hide. I practised
detachment. I learned how to smile pleasantly while, under
the table, I stuck a fork into the back of my hand. I became
not merely impenetrable, but a virtuoso of deceit. Needless
to say, at that stage nobody told me anything: and it wasn't
pleasure I was after, it was knowledge. But when, in the
interests of furthering that knowledge, I told my confessor
I'd done 'everything', his reaction was so appalled, I began
to get a sense of how extreme pleasure might be. No sooner
had I made this discovery than my mother announced my
marriage: so I was able to contain my curiosity and arrived
in Monsieur de Merteuil's arms a virgin. All in all, Merteuil
gave me little cause for complaint: and the minute I began
to find him something of a nuisance, he very tactfully
died. I used my year of mourning to complete my studies:
I consulted the strictest moralists to learn how to appear;
philosophers to find out what to think; and novelists to see
what I could get away with. And finally I was well placed to
perfect my techniques.

Valmont Describe them.

Merteuil Only flirt with those you intend to refuse: then you acquire a reputation for invincibility, whilst slipping safely away with the lover of your choice. A poor choice is less dangerous than an obvious choice. Always be sure they think they're the only one. Win or die.

Valmont smiles. He looks at her for a moment.

Valmont These principles are infallible, are they?

Merteuil When I want a man, I have him; when he wants to tell, he finds he can't. That's the whole story.

Valmont And was that our story?

Merteuil pauses before answering.

Merteuil I wanted you before we'd even met. My self-esteem demanded it. Then, when you began to pursue me . . . I wanted you so badly. It's the only one of my notions has ever got the better of me. Single combat.

Valmont Thank you.

He's about to say more, but is interrupted by the arrival of Merteuil's Majordomo, escorting the Chevalier Danceny, a Knight of Malta, an eager and handsome young man of about twenty. Danceny hurries over and bows to kiss Merteuil's hand. Then he acknowledges Valmont.

Danceny Vicomte.

Valmont My dear young man. How good to see you again.

Danceny turns back to Merteuil, speaks a trifle breathlessly.

Danceny I'm so sorry to be late, Madame.

Merteuil Very nearly too late.

But looking up at his sincerely repentant expression, she softens.

As you know, Mademoiselle de Volanges . . .

Danceny It gives me such pleasure to hear her name spoken, Madame.

Merteuil Yes, yes, quite. As I was saying, Mademoiselle de Volanges has done me the honour of making me her confidante and counsellor in this matter which concerns you both.

Danceny She could hardly have chosen more wisely.

Merteuil Yes, well, be that as it may, I felt very strongly that in this situation, which is exceedingly delicate, you too might find it beneficial to be able to confide in someone sympathetic, a person of experience: and the Vicomte de Valmont, who is known to you as well as being an old friend of mine and a man of unswerving discretion, seems to me an ideal choice. And, should you agree, he's very kindly consented to devote himself to your interests.

A frown crosses Valmont's face, but by the time Danceny, who for his part seems slightly flustered by this offer, turns to him, it's vanished.

Danceny Well . . .

Valmont Perhaps it is my reputation which is causing you to hesitate: if so, I think I can assure you that a man's own mistakes are not necessarily a guide to his faculty for objective judgement.

Danceny No, of course not, I certainly wouldn't have the impudence, no, it's . . . the fact is, this is not a conventional intrigue with the aim of . . . that's to say, my love and respect.

Valmont We're not dealing, you mean, with a frivolous coquette or a bored wife?

Danceny Precisely. A person like Mademoiselle de Volanges must be treated with the utmost consideration. And my own position has certain weaknesses, of which I'm only too bitterly aware. Her great fortune, for example, compared to my own precarious condition . . .

Valmont Naturally, there would be no excuse for trying to manoeuvre her into such a pass that she would be forced to marry you, that would be quite wrong.

Danceny You do understand how I feel.

Merteuil Of course he does, what did I tell you?

Danceny You see, I'm quite happy with things as they are, as long as she consents to see me, to continue with the music lessons.

Valmont Ah, the music lessons.

The Majordomo reappears and crosses the room to murmur to Merteuil. She gives him some instructions in an undertone and he bows and leaves.

Merteuil I'm sorry, Chevalier, but I'm afraid you must leave. Madame de Volanges has just been announced. You see now why I was concerned at your late arrival.

Danceny Maybe this would be a good opportunity for me to pay my respects and hope to . . .

Merteuil I really think at this juncture, Monsieur Danceny, it would be prudent for you not to be found here. That is if you want me to be of any effective assistance in the future.

During this speech, a Footman has entered.

Danceny Of course, whatever you think fit.

Merteuil Goodbye, Chevalier. My man will show you to a side exit.

Danceny kisses her hand in hurried farewell. Valmont takes his arm as he crosses to the door.

Valmont I have to go to Versailles tomorrow, I don't know if you'd care to accompany me.

Danceny I'd like that very much.

Valmont Good, I'll send a carriage for you at nine.

Danceny vanishes with the Footman. Valmont turns back to Merteuil.

So this is the scene you have planned for me?

Merteuil If you'd care to go behind the screen.

She indicates a screen in a corner of the room, a trace of anxious impatience in her voice.

Valmont I think you might have consulted me before offering my services as general factotum to that exasperating boy. I don't find lovers' complaints remotely entertaining outside of the Opéra.

Merteuil I was sure that if anyone could help him . . .

Valmont Help? He doesn't need help, he needs hindrances: if he has to climb over enough of them, he might inadvertently fall on top of her.

Merteuil I'll see what I can do: now, Vicomte, the screen.

Valmont starts moving towards it, then hesitates.

Valmont Are you sure I shouldn't confront her? Give her some evidence for those rude letters?

Merteuil Quick.

Valmont moves swiftly and is only just behind the screen in time not to be seen by Mme de Volanges, as she's shown in by the Majordomo. Merteuil, who has assumed a grave expression, rises to greet her, kissing her on both cheeks.

Volanges Your note said it was urgent . . .

Merteuil It's days now, I haven't been able to think about anything else, I couldn't decide what to do for the best.

Finally I saw there was no escaping the fact it was my plain duty to tell you. Please sit down.

Mme de Volanges, now decidedly uneasy, does so, as Merteuil paces to and fro, looking anguished.

As you know, in recent weeks, Cécile has been kind enough to accept my friendship and, I believe, bestow on me her own.

Volanges Yes, of course, she's devoted to you.

Merteuil This is what makes this duty doubly difficult to perform.

Volanges This has something to do with Cécile?

Merteuil I may be wrong; I pray Heaven I am.

She pauses again; by now, Mme de Volanges is thoroughly alarmed.

Volanges Go on.

Merteuil takes a deep breath.

Merteuil I have reason to believe that a, how can I describe it, a dangerous liaison has sprung up between your daughter and the Chevalier Danceny.

Silence. Mme de Volanges is dumbfounded and so, should he be visible behind the screen, is Valmont. But it takes only a few seconds for Mme de Volanges to recover her equilibrium.

Volanges No, no, that's completely absurd. Cécile is still a child, she understands nothing of these things; and Danceny is an entirely respectable young man.

Merteuil If you were to be right, no one would be happier than I.

Volanges Naturally, they've never been together unchaperoned, generally by me and often by you.

Merteuil Precisely, that's when I first formed the impression that something was passing between them: the way they looked at each other.

Volanges I'm sure it's merely their feeling for the music.

Merteuil Perhaps so. But there was one other thing. Tell me, does Cécile have a great many correspondents?

Volanges She writes, I suppose, an average number of letters. Relatives, friends from the convent . . . Why?

Merteuil I went into her room at the beginning of this week, I simply knocked and entered without waiting for a reply, and she was stuffing a letter into the left-hand drawer of her bureau, in which, I couldn't help noticing, there seemed to be a large number of similar letters.

Silence. Then Mme de Volanges rises to her feet.

I hope you don't think me interfering.

Volanges Not at all.

Merteuil And I do hope, if, God forbid, you do discover anything compromising, you won't tell Cécile it was I who was responsible. I would hate to forfeit her trust, and if there is to be a period of difficulty, I would like to think my advice might be of some use to her.

Volanges Of course.

Merteuil rings. Mme de Volanges stands there, still in a state of mild shock.

Merteuil Would you think it impertinent if I were to make another suggestion?

Volanges No, no.

Merteuil If my recollection is correct, I overheard you saying to the Vicomte de Valmont that his aunt had invited you to stay at her château.

Volanges She has, yes, repeatedly.

Merteuil A spell in the country might be the very thing until all this blows over.

The Majordomo has arrived and Merteuil beckons him over. Mme de Volanges meanwhile is lost in thought. She looks up, frowning.

Volanges Isn't the Vicomte staying there at the moment?

Merteuil I understand he's returned to Paris.

She embraces Mme de Volanges warmly.

I expect I've imagined the whole thing and tomorrow we'll be able to laugh at my stupidity. If so, I hope you'll be able to forgive me.

Volanges My dear, I shall always be more than grateful for your concern.

They part; and Mme de Volanges moves slowly out of the room, bowed down with care, following the Majordomo. Because of her slow progress, Valmont emerges from behind the screen before she's disappeared, to Merteuil's alarm. But Mme de Volanges doesn't look back and Valmont can't resist making faces at her retreating back, causing Merteuil to hiss at him.

Merteuil Stop it.

Valmont So, you understand I've returned to Paris?

Merteuil You asked for hindrances.

Valmont You're a genuinely wicked woman.

Merteuil And you wanted a chance to make my cousin suffer.

Valmont I can't resist you.

Merteuil I've made it easy for you.

Valmont But all this is most inconvenient: the Comtesse de Beaulieu has invited me to stay.

Merteuil Well, you'll have to put her off.

Valmont The Comtesse has promised me extensive use of her gardens. It seems her husband's fingers are not as green as they once were.

Merteuil Maybe not. But from what I hear, all his friends are gardeners.

Valmont Is that so?

Merteuil You want your revenge: I want my revenge. I'm afraid there's really only one place you can go.

Valmont Back to Auntie, eh?

Merteuil Back to Auntie. Where you can also pursue that other matter. You have some evidence to procure, have you not?

Valmont Don't you think it would be a generous gesture, show a proper confidence in my abilities, I mean, to take that evidence for granted, and . . . ?

Merteuil I need it in writing, Vicomte.

He gives her his most charming smile, but it leaves her unmoved.

And now you must leave me.

Valmont Must I? Why?

Merteuil Because I'm hungry.

Valmont Yes, I've quite an appetite myself.

Merteuil Then go home and eat.

Silence. Then he crosses to her and lingeringly kisses her hand.

In writing.

Valmont smiles, turns and strides away.

SIX

*A week later. After lunch. The salon in Mme de
Rosemonde's château. Mme de Tourvel is stretched out on
the chaise-longue, ashen; Cécile sits in the window, working
at her tapestry; Mme de Rosemonde and Mme de Volanges
sit at the card table; and only Valmont is on his feet, moving
around the room, his eye roving from Mme de Tourvel to
Cécile and back again.*

Rosemonde You'll be pleased to hear, my dear, that
Armand is on his feet again and back at work.

Valmont Who?

Rosemonde Monsieur Armand, you remember, whose
family you helped so generously.

Valmont Oh, yes.

*He comes to rest and sits down, his eye fixed now on
Mme de Tourvel. When she looks at him, he looks away
for a few seconds at Cécile, and is gratified to notice,
when he looks back at Mme de Tourvel, that she's still
looking at him, although she looks away again, in some
confusion, the minute he catches her out.*

Rosemonde We've been keeping an eye on things while
you've been away: I must say he never ceases to sing your
praises.

She turns to Mme de Volanges.

When my nephew was last staying here, we discovered quite
by chance that he had been down to the village and . . .

*Valmont suddenly rises to his feet, still staring at Mme de
Tourvel.*

Valmont Are you feeling all right, Madame?

Momentary confusion.

I'm sorry to interrupt you, Aunt, it seemed to me all of a sudden that Madame de Tourvel didn't look at all well.

Tourvel I'm . . . no, I'm quite all right.

By now, Mme de Rosemonde and Mme de Volanges are on their feet and hurrying towards Mme de Tourvel. As they bear down on her, Valmont turns towards Cécile, who's still sitting, needle poised, in the window, and deftly throws a letter into her lap. She's so amazed by this, she sits there for a moment, gaping: until she grasps the significance of Valmont's impatient gestures, tosses her tapestry aside and stuffs the letter in her pocket. Finally, again at a gesture from Valmont, she moves towards the chaise-longue, exhibiting polite concern and standing, next to Valmont, at a respectful distance from the centre of attention, Mme de Tourvel.

Rosemonde You do look dreadfully pale, my dear.

Tourvel I'm all right.

Volanges Perhaps you need some air. Do you feel constricted in any way?

Tourvel No, really.

Valmont I feel sure Madame de Volanges is right, as usual. A turn around the grounds, perhaps.

Rosemonde Yes, yes, a little walk in the garden, it's not too cool, I think.

Tourvel Well, perhaps . . .

Volanges Come along, my dear, we'll all accompany you.

Tourvel I'll be quite happy on my own.

Valmont You'll have to excuse me, ladies, but I think you're right to insist on chaperoning Madame.

Mme de Tourvel is wrong-footed by this: she frowns slightly in puzzlement and allows a shawl to be wrapped

*around her shoulders as she's propelled towards the
French windows by Mme de Rosemonde and Mme de
Volanges.*

Rosemonde Fresh air will do you the world of good.

Volanges The meal was somewhat heavy, perhaps . . .

Rosemonde I don't believe that can be the cause, Solange is
an excellent cook.

*During this exchange, Cécile has gathered up her shawl
and made to follow the others. As she's spreading it
across her shoulders, however, she's startled to find it
tugged away from her by Valmont, who drops it on
a chair and simultaneously murmurs to her between
clenched teeth.*

Valmont Come back for it.

*She frowns at him for a moment, then follows the still-
clucking ladies, who are now supporting Mme de Tourvel
on either side, out into the garden. Hiatus. Valmont
moves around the room, apparently well pleased.
Presently, Cécile reappears and stands hesitantly just
inside the windows. Valmont picks up her shawl and
strides towards her.*

I don't want to arouse suspicion, Mademoiselle, so I must
be brief and I must ask you to pay close attention to what
I say. As you've no doubt guessed, the letter I gave you is
from our friend, the Chevalier Danceny.

Cécile Yes, I thought so, Monsieur.

Valmont And as I'm sure you're also aware, the handing
over of letters is a far from easy matter to accomplish.
I can't very well create a diversion every day.

Cécile And Maman has taken away my paper and pens.

Valmont Right, now listen carefully: there are two large
cupboards in the antechamber next to your room. In the

left-hand cupboard, you will find a supply of paper, pens and ink.

Cécile Oh, thank you!

Valmont I suggest you return the Chevalier's letters to me, when you've read them, for safe-keeping.

Cécile Must I?

Valmont It would be wise.

At this point, Valmont produces a key from his waistcoat pocket.

Now, this key resembles the key to your bedroom, which I happen to know is kept in your mother's room, on the mantelpiece, tied with a blue ribbon. Take it, attach the blue ribbon to it and put it in the place of your bedroom key, which you will then bring to me. I'll be able to get a copy cut within two hours, I'll return you the original and you can put it back in your mother's room. Then I'll be able to collect your letters and deliver Danceny's without any complications.

He hands the key to Cécile, who takes it dubiously.

Oh, and on the shelf below the writing paper, you'll find a feather and a small bottle of oil, so that you can oil the lock and hinges on your bedroom door.

Cécile Are you sure, Monsieur? I'm not sure it would be right . . .

Valmont How else are we going to manage this? Your mother never lets you out of her sight. You really must trust me, my dear.

Cécile Well, I know Monsieur Danceny has every confidence in you . . .

Valmont Believe me, Mademoiselle, if there's one thing I can't abide, it's deceitfulness. It's only my very warm friendship for Danceny which would ever make me consider such methods.

Cécile smiles uncertainly and puts the key away. She stands there, obviously racked with indecision.

And now I suggest you rejoin your mama and the others before they send out a search party.

Cécile Yes, Monsieur. Thank you, Monsieur.

She turns and hurries back into the garden with her shawl. Valmont watches her go, thoughtful.

Valmont My pleasure.

He moves over to an armchair and sinks into it, picks up a book from the arm of the chair, finds his place and settles to read. The lights change. It's early evening now, and Valmont, still reading, looks up as Mme de Tourvel comes into the room. She freezes as soon as she sees Valmont, who puts down his book and rises to his feet.

I trust you're feeling a little better, Madame.

Tourvel If I had felt ill, Monsieur, it would not be difficult to guess who was responsible.

Valmont You can't mean me. Do you?

Tourvel You promised to leave here.

Valmont And I did.

Tourvel Then how can you be insensitive enough to return uninvited and without warning?

Valmont I find myself obliged to attend to some urgent business in the area: in which, moreover, my aunt is crucially involved.

Tourvel I only hope it can be dealt with promptly.

By now, Mme de Tourvel has cautiously moved closer to the centre of the room. As the conversation continues,

Valmont contrives, imperceptibly, to manoeuvre himself between her and the door.

Valmont Why are you so angry with me?

Tourvel I'm not angry. Although, since you gave me a solemn undertaking not to offend me when you wrote and then in your very first letter spoke of nothing but the disorders of love, I'm certainly entitled to be.

Valmont I was away almost three weeks and wrote to you only three times. Since I was quite unable to think about anything but you, some might say I showed heroic restraint.

Tourvel Not in so far as you persisted in writing about your love, despite my pleas for you not to do so.

Valmont It's true: I couldn't find the strength to obey you.

Tourvel You claim to think there's some connection between what you call love and happiness: I can't believe that there is.

Valmont In these circumstances, I agree. When the love is unrequited . . .

Tourvel As it must be. You know it's impossible for me to reciprocate your feelings; and even if I did, it could only cause me suffering, without making you any the happier.

Valmont I believe I've done everything you've asked of me.

Tourvel You've done nothing of the sort.

Valmont I left here when you wanted me to.

Tourvel And you came back.

Silence, as Valmont searches for a way forward, momentarily at a loss.

I've offered you my friendship, Monsieur. It's the only thing I can give you: why can't you accept it?

Valmont I could pretend to: but that would be dishonest.

Tourvel You're not answering my question.

Valmont The man I used to be would have been content with friendship; and set about trying to turn it to his advantage. But I've changed now: and I can't conceal from you that I love you tenderly, passionately and above all, respectfully. So how am I to demote myself to the tepid position of friend?

Valmont's strategy has paid off, because at this moment Mme de Tourvel decides to leave the room and finds the way blocked.

And in any case, you're no longer even pretending to show friendship.

Tourvel What do you mean?

Valmont Well, is this friendly?

Tourvel You can hardly expect me to stay here and listen to the expression of sentiments you know very well I can only find insulting.

Valmont I think you're misunderstanding me: I know you can bestow on me nothing more than your friendship, for which, by the way, I'm profoundly grateful. In the same way, I can feel nothing less for you than love. We both know this is the true position: can't we simply acknowledge it? I don't see why recognition of the truth should lose me your friendship. Openness and honesty scarcely deserve to be punished, don't you agree?

Tourvel You are adept, Monsieur, at framing questions which preclude the answer no. Your honesty or otherwise is not at issue. The point is, surely, that I was weak enough to be persuaded to grant you a favour you should never have obtained; and furthermore I did this under certain conditions, not a single one of which you have observed. Naturally, I feel you've exploited my good faith.

Valmont What can I say to reassure you? How can you be afraid of me when, because I love you, your happiness is

far more important to me than my own? You've made me a
better person: you mustn't now undo your handiwork.

Tourvel I've no wish to: but I must ask whether you're
going to leave the room or let me pass.

Valmont But why?

Tourvel Because I find this conversation distressing. I can't
seem to make you understand what I mean; and I've no
wish to hear what you invariably get round to saying.

Valmont Very well, I shall leave you in possession of the
field.

Tourvel Thank you.

Valmont But look: I shall expedite my business, as you ask.
But we are to be living under the same roof, at least for a few
days; could we not contrive to tolerate it when fate throws us
together? Surely we don't have to try to avoid each other?

Silence. Valmont waits.

Tourvel Of course not. Providing you adhere to my few
simple rules.

Valmont I shall obey you in this as in everything. I wish
you knew me well enough to recognise how much you've
changed me. My friends in Paris remarked on it at once. I've
become the soul of consideration, charitable, conscientious,
more celibate than a monk . . .

Tourvel More celibate?

Valmont Well, you know, the stories one hears in Paris.

Pause.

It's all due to your influence, I have you to thank for it. And
now, good evening.

*He bows deep and turns away, begins moving towards
the door.*

Tourvel Monsieur . . . ?

Valmont What?

She looks at him for a moment, troubled: then shakes her head.

Tourvel Nothing.

Valmont turns away, permits himself a private smile and leaves. Mme de Tourvel stands for a long time, not moving, locked in some personal struggle.

SEVEN

A fortnight later. The middle of the night. Cécile's bedroom in the château. Darkness. Cécile is fast asleep. After a while, there's the sound of a key in the lock. It operates smoothly and Valmont lets himself quietly into the room. He's wearing a dressing gown and carrying a dark lantern. He crosses to the bed and stands for a moment, contemplating the still-sleeping Cécile.

In a far corner, seated at her desk in a pool of light, is Mme de Merteuil. She's writing a letter; we hear her voice.

Merteuil 'You don't know how lucky you are to have me as a friend, I'm your Good Fairy! You want to revenge yourself on a woman who has done you harm: one word from me and there you are, on the spot, able to strike at your leisure. Except, why do I get the sense you're being a little too leisurely? I shall have to come and see for myself.'

It's as if Valmont can hear her provocative tone: he gestures, as if to say, he's at last following orders. He puts the lantern down carefully and, after some thought, leans forward and very gently eases back the covers. Cécile's eyes open, wide and staring. Valmont smiles down at her and speaks in a whisper.

49

Valmont Nothing to worry about.

He removes his hand; she continues to gape at him.

Cécile Have you . . . have you brought a letter?

Valmont No. Oh, no.

Cécile Then what . . . ?

Instead of answering, he leans over to kiss her. Her response is to dive across the bed to reach for the bell-pull. Valmont dives onto the bed in his turn, grasping her wrist just in time. They grapple fiercely and silently for a moment, until he manages to subdue her.

Valmont You mustn't do that. What are you going to tell your mother when she arrives? How will you explain the fact that I have your key? If I tell her I'm here at your invitation, I have a feeling she'll believe me.

Cécile What do you want?

Valmont Well, I don't know, what do you think?

Cécile doesn't answer; she looks frightened.

I just want you to give me a kiss.

Cécile A kiss?

Valmont That's all.

Cécile And then will you go?

Valmont Then I'll go.

Cécile Promise?

Valmont Whatever you say.

Cécile flops back on the pillow, with a slight groan and speaks, almost inaudibly.

Cécile All right.

Valmont leans over her and gives her a long kiss. After a while he pulls away, but makes no move to disengage himself further.

All right?

Valmont Very nice.

Cécile No, I mean, will you go now?

Valmont Oh, I don't think so.

Cécile But you promised.

Valmont I promised to go when you gave me a kiss. You didn't give me a kiss. I gave you a kiss. Not the same thing at all.

Silence. Cécile peers at him miserably. He looks back at her, calmly waiting.

Cécile And if I give you a kiss . . . ?

Valmont That's what I said.

Cécile You really promise?

She kisses him; the kiss, at first tentative, then turns into something more elaborate. Eventually, Valmont disengages.

Valmont Let's just get ourselves more comfortable, shall we?

EIGHT

It's the following day, 1 October. The low afternoon sun slants in through the windows of the salon in Mme de Rosemonde's château. At first, the room is empty: then Cécile appears, arm in arm with Mme de Merteuil, who seems almost to be supporting her. Cécile looks exhausted and distraught; Merteuil, solicitous.

Merteuil My dear, I really can't help you unless you tell me what's troubling you.

Cécile I can't, I just can't.

Merteuil I thought we'd agreed not to keep any secrets from one another.

Cécile I'm so unhappy.

She bursts into tears. Merteuil takes her in her arms and soothes her mechanically, her expression, as long as it's not seen by Cécile, bored and impatient.

Everything's gone wrong since the day Maman found Danceny's letters.

Merteuil Yes, that was very stupid of you. How could you have let that happen?

Cécile Someone must have told her, she went straight to my bureau and opened the drawer I was keeping them in.

Merteuil Who could have done such a thing?

Cécile It must have been my chambermaid . . .

Merteuil Or your confessor perhaps?

Cécile Oh, no, surely not.

Merteuil You can't always trust those people, my dear.

Cécile That's terrible.

Merteuil But today, what is the matter today?

Cécile You'll be angry with me.

Merteuil Are you sure you don't want me to be angry with you?

Cécile looks up at Merteuil, surprised by the acuteness of this idea.

Come along.

Cécile I don't know how to speak the words.

Merteuil Perhaps I am beginning to get angry.

She's spoken quietly; and now there's a long silence. Finally, Cécile takes a deep breath.

Cécile Last night . . .

Merteuil Yes.

Cécile So that we could exchange letters to and from Danceny without arousing suspicion, I gave Monsieur de Valmont the key to my bedroom . . .

Merteuil Yes.

Cécile And last night he used it. I thought he'd just come to bring me a letter. But he hadn't. And by the time I realised what he had come for, it was, well, it was too late to stop him . . .

She bursts into tears again; but this time Merteuil doesn't take her in her arms. Instead, she considers her coolly for a moment before speaking.

Merteuil You mean to tell me you're upset because Monsieur de Valmont has taught you something you've undoubtedly been dying to learn?

Cécile's tears are cut off and she looks up in shock.

Cécile What?

Merteuil And am I to understand that what generally brings a girl to her senses has deprived you of yours?

Cécile I thought you'd be horrified.

Merteuil Tell me: you resisted him, did you?

Cécile Of course I did, as much as I could.

Merteuil But he forced you?

Cécile It wasn't that exactly, but I found it almost impossible to defend myself.

Merteuil Why was that? Did he tie you up?

Cécile No, no, but he has a way of putting things, you just can't think of an answer.

Merteuil Not even no?

Silence. Cécile seems, once again, trembling on the edge of tears.

Cécile I'm so ashamed.

Merteuil speaks with sudden melancholy.

Merteuil You'll find the shame is like the pain: you only feel it once.

Cécile And this morning it was terrible. As soon as I saw Maman, I couldn't help it, I burst into tears.

Merteuil I'm surprised you missed the opportunity to bring the whole thing to a rousing climax by confessing all. Then you'd be packing your bags to go back to the convent for the rest of your life.

Cécile What am I going to do?

Merteuil You really want my advice?

Cécile Please.

Merteuil considers a moment.

Merteuil Allow Monsieur de Valmont to continue your instruction. Convince your mother you have forgotten Danceny. And raise no objection to the marriage.

Cécile gapes at her, bewildered.

Cécile With Monsieur de Gercourt?

Merteuil When it comes to marriage one man is as good as the next; and even the least accommodating is less trouble than a mother.

Cécile But what about Danceny?

Merteuil He seems patient enough; and once you're married, you should be able to see him without undue difficulty.

Cécile I thought you once said to me, I'm sure you did, one evening at the Opéra, that once I was married, I would have to be faithful to my husband.

Merteuil Your mind must have been wandering, you must have been listening to the opera.

Cécile So, are you saying I'm going to have to do that with three different men?

Merteuil I'm saying, you stupid little girl, that provided you take a few elementary precautions, you can do it, or not, with as many men as you like, as often as you like, in as many different ways as you like. Our sex has few enough advantages, you may as well make the most of those you have. Now here comes your mama so remember what I've said and, above all, no more snivelling.

Cécile Yes, Madame.

And by now, Mme de Volanges is more or less upon them. She acknowledges Merteuil perfunctorily, but her anxious attention is directed almost entirely towards Cécile, whose expression is now profoundly thoughtful.

Volanges How are you feeling now, my dear?

Cécile Oh, much better, thank you, Maman.

Volanges You look so tired. I think you should go to bed.

Cécile No, really, I've . . .

Merteuil I think you should do as your mother suggests.
We can arrange for something to be brought to your room.
I'm sure it would do you good.

Cécile Well. Perhaps you're right, Madame.

*She curtsies to Merteuil and kisses her mother on both
cheeks.*

Volanges I'll come up and see you later on.

*Cécile makes a demure exit, watched by the others. When
she's left the room, Mme de Volanges turns back to
Merteuil.*

You have such a very good influence on her.

Merteuil I like to think so. But what do you suppose is the
matter?

Volanges Didn't she tell you?

Merteuil No, we merely spoke of how she was enjoying the
country.

Volanges That makes me even more certain of the cause
of her unhappiness. She's pining for that young man. I'm
afraid it's beginning to affect her health.

Merteuil Do you think so?

*Mme de Volanges sighs deeply. Then she turns decisively
to Merteuil.*

Volanges My dear, I really feel I need your advice.

Merteuil My dear friend, please, I'd be proud to think
I could be of any help to you.

Volanges Perhaps I should break off Cécile's engagement
with Monsieur de Gercourt.

Merteuil's head jerks up.

He is no doubt a better match than Danceny, but the family,
after all, is not decisively superior. Danceny is not rich,
of course: but I dare say Cécile is rich enough for both of
them. And the most important thing is that they love each
other. Don't you agree?

Silence. Merteuil is thinking fast.

You think I'm wrong?

Merteuil I have every confidence that your eventual
decision will be the right one. If I were able to take a more
objective view of the situation, it would only be because, in
this case, I am not affected by the altogether praiseworthy
emotion of maternal love.

Volanges Please go on, I do rely on your judgement.

Merteuil Well. To say this young man is entitled to your
daughter just because of his passion for her is a little like
saying a thief is entitled to your money. I'm not at all sure
how appropriate an emotion love is, particularly within
marriage. I believe friendship, trust and mutual respect are
infinitely more important.

Volanges And you don't approve of Danceny?

Merteuil I know money isn't everything: but will sixty
thousand a year really be sufficient to maintain the kind
of establishment Cécile will be obliged to run, even as
Madame Danceny? Of course, I wouldn't dream of
suggesting in any way that Danceny has allowed himself to
be influenced by financial considerations . . .

Volanges But?

Merteuil Precisely.

Silence. Mme de Volanges reflects.
    *Valmont has entered the room. He bows, as the ladies
turn to him.*

Valmont Mesdames.

Volanges If you'll excuse me, Monsieur, I must go and make arrangements for some supper to be taken up to my daughter.

Valmont Oh, is she indisposed?

Volanges For the moment.

Valmont The young have such miraculous powers of recuperation. I'm sure she'll soon be back in the saddle. Tell her I hope so, at least.

Volanges Thank you, Monsieur.

She leaves the room briskly. Valmont watches her go and then turns back to grin at Merteuil.

Valmont You see, she can hardly bear to be in the same room with me.

Merteuil But I gather you've had your revenge. Well done.

Valmont So you know?

Merteuil The little one could hardly wait to tell me.

Valmont A favourable report, I trust?

Merteuil On the contrary, Vicomte, if I hadn't spoken to her sharply, I think on your next visit you'd have found her door bolted as well as locked.

Valmont You surprise me. I was malicious enough to use no more strength than could easily be resisted.

Merteuil Still, for some reason she seems to think it was rather an underhand approach.

Valmont I'd been postponing it, to tell you the truth. But when you wrote to say you'd be arriving today, I wanted to be able to afford you some amusement at least.

She considers him for a moment.

Merteuil I'm beginning to have my doubts about you, Vicomte. Do you really deserve your reputation? You see, the real reason I consented to spend a night at this lugubrious address was that I was hoping to be shown some tear-stained bit of paper.

Valmont Ah.

Merteuil But I can only assume from what you've been saying that no such document exists.

Valmont No.

Merteuil Probably just as well, no doubt you're exhausted after last night's exertions.

Valmont I think you know me better than that.

Merteuil Well, I wonder. Can you account for this extraordinary dilatoriness?

Valmont Lugubrious or not, I haven't experienced a moment's boredom in all the weeks I've spent here. I appreciate you may have excellent reasons for your impatience, but you mustn't try to deprive me of my simple pleasures. I've explained to you before how much I enjoy watching the battle between love and virtue.

Merteuil What concerns me is that you appear to enjoy watching it more than you used to enjoy winning it.

Valmont All in good time.

Merteuil The century is drawing to its close, Vicomte.

Valmont It's true that she's resisted me for more than two months now; and that's very nearly a record. But I really don't want to hurry things. We go for a walk together almost every day: a little further every time down the path that has no turning. She's accepted my love; I've accepted her friendship; we're both aware how little there is to choose between them. Her eyes are closing. Every step she tries to take away from the inevitable conclusion brings her a little nearer to it. Hopes and fears, passion and suspense: even if you were in the theatre, what more could you ask?

Merteuil An audience?

Valmont But you: you're my audience. And when Gercourt is married and Madame de Tourvel eventually collapses, we shall tell everyone, shall we not? And the story will spread much faster than the plot of the latest play; and I've no doubt it will be much better received.

Merteuil I hope you're right, Vicomte. I wish I could share your confidence.

Valmont I'm only sorry our agreement does not relate to the task you set me rather than the task I set myself.

Merteuil I am grateful, of course: but that would have been almost insultingly simple. One does not applaud the tenor for clearing his throat.

Valmont You're right, how could one possibly compare them . . . ?

He breaks off as Mme de Rosemonde comes into the room, followed by Mme de Tourvel. Mme de Rosemonde bustles over to Merteuil to embrace her: Merteuil responds convincingly, but it's clear she has immediately registered the look which passes between Valmont and Mme de Tourvel, a look that indicates that there has indeed been some progress in their relationship.

Rosemonde I'm so delighted you could manage to visit us, my dear, even if only for such a short time.

Merteuil I wish I could stay longer, Madame, but my husband's estate . . .

Rosemonde Do you know, it feels only yesterday that you were last here, with your dear husband. Such a kind and such a vigorous man, who could have imagined . . . Ah, well . . .

*Merteuil, who is centrally placed, has been watching
Mme de Tourvel and, more particularly, Valmont, who
really is lost in contemplation of Mme de Tourvel. She
doesn't like what she sees: it clearly troubles her, even
though, after only the briefest pause, she manages a civil
reply to Mme de Rosemonde.*

Merteuil Yes, Madame, there's no denying that life is
frighteningly unpredictable.

NINE

*Cécile's bedroom. It's very late the following night and
Cécile is in her nightdress, but she's not in bed. She's sitting
at her dressing table, her expression thoughtful. She looks
up as there's a soft tap at the door.*

Cécile Come in.

*Valmont appears with his dark lantern. Cécile considers
him coolly.*

Valmont You don't seem surprised to see me.

Cécile I would have been surprised not to see you.

Valmont is taken aback, though not displeased.

Valmont I was going to make a suggestion . . .

Cécile I imagine you were.

Again, Valmont is momentarily derailed.

Valmont Your mother's room is uncomfortably close, is it
not? I thought if we were to move over to my room at the
far end of the corridor, we wouldn't have to . . . restrain
ourselves in any way.

Cécile is already on her feet.

And my mattress is a little harder.

Cécile Is that good?

Valmont Yes, that's very good.

Valmont, still processing this new version of Cécile, leads her along the corridor to his room. Once through the door, Cécile prods the mattress to test his assertion. She starts to take off her nightdress, but he puts out a hand to restrain her.

The first thing you must learn is that there is no necessity whatsoever for haste.

He reaches out to caress her.

Tell me, what did Madame de Merteuil have to say about me?

Cécile She said you were a dangerous man to try to leave.

Valmont Really?

Cécile And she also said you could teach me a great many skills.

Valmont Well, certainly: education is never a waste; and, as with every other science, the first principle is to make sure you call everything by its proper name.

Cécile I don't see why you have to talk at all.

Valmont Without the correct polite vocabulary, how can you indicate what you would like me to do or make me an offer of something I might find agreeable?

Cécile You mean . . . I could tell you . . . what I'm thinking about?

Valmont Of course. And then I would be able to do my best to . . . fulfill that inclination. If I do my work adequately, I would like to think you'll be able to surprise Monsieur de Gercourt on your wedding night.

Cécile Would he be pleased?

Valmont Well, of course, he'll merely assume your mama has done her duty and fully briefed you.

Cécile bursts out laughing.

Cécile Maman couldn't possibly talk about anything of the sort.

Valmont I can't think why. She was, after all, at one time one of the most notorious young women in Paris.

Cécile Maman?

Valmont Certainly. More noted for her enthusiasm than her ability, if I remember rightly, but nonetheless renowned. There was a famous occasion, oh, many years before you were born, this would have been, when she went to stay with the Comtesse de Beaulieu, who tactfully gave her a room between your father's and that of a Monsieur de Vressac, who was her acknowledged lover at the time. Yet in spite of these careful arrangements, she contrived to spend the night with a third party.

Cécile laughs again.

Cécile I can't believe that; it's just gossip.

Valmont No, no, I assure you it's true.

Cécile How do you know?

Valmont This third party was myself.

Cécile's jaw drops. For a moment she stares at Valmont, horrified. He returns a bland smile and, all of a sudden, she can't resist smiling herself. Valmont turns back the covers.

Well, we can return to this subject later. During the intervals. You asked me if Monsieur de Gercourt would be pleased with your abilities; more to the point, you'll be pleased. Very pleased.

He reaches out and puts a hand round her, drawing her to him. He caresses her thoughtfully.

Now. I think we might begin with one or two Latin terms.

TEN

Late the following evening. Mme de Tourvel lingers alone in the salon in the château. The card table is out, still scattered with cards. Mme de Tourvel, drifting somewhat aimlessly, glancing at the door from time to time, seems to have no particular reason for being in the room. She starts, however, and moves briskly to the table to begin tidying away the cards as soon as Valmont, looking elegant but frail, appears in the doorway.

Valmont You're alone, Madame.

He advances into the room as Mme de Tourvel answers shakily.

Tourvel The others have all decided on an early night. Mademoiselle de Volanges in particular seems to be quite exhausted.

Valmont I must admit to being rather tired myself.

He arrives at the card table.

May I help you with these?

He reaches for some cards, brushing her hand in the process, causing her to let go of the cards she's already collected.

Tourvel No, I'm sure the servants will . . .

She moves away from the table in some confusion, heading in the general direction of the chaise-longue. Valmont watches her.

Valmont I'm glad to have found you, I very much missed our walk today.

Tourvel Yes . . .

Valmont I fear with the weather as it is, we can look forward to very few more of them.

Tourvel This heavy rain is surely exceptional.

Valmont But in a week I shall have concluded my business.

Tourvel I see.

She stops, affected by this news. Valmont begins, very gradually, to move closer.

Valmont I may, however, be unable to bring myself to leave.

Mme de Tourvel turns to face him, beset by conflicting emotions.

Tourvel You must!

Valmont Are you still so anxious to get rid of me?

Tourvel You know the answer to that. I must rely on your integrity and generosity. I want to be able to be grateful to you.

Valmont Forgive me if I say I don't want your gratitude. Gratitude I can get from strangers; what I want from you is something altogether deeper.

Tourvel I know God is punishing me for my pride. I was so certain nothing like this could ever happen to me.

Valmont Nothing like what?

Tourvel I can't . . .

Valmont Do you mean love? Is love what you mean?

He's beside her now and takes her hand. She starts, but does not remove her hand.

Tourvel Don't ask me, you promised not to speak of it.

Valmont But I must know. I need this consolation at least.

Silence. Mme de Tourvel still holds Valmont's hand, but cannot bring herself to look at him.

Tourvel I can't . . . don't you see? . . . It's impossible.

Valmont I understand, I don't want you to say anything, but I must know, I must know if you love me, don't speak, you don't have to speak, I just want you to look at me. Just look. That's all I ask.

Long silence. Then, slowly, Mme de Tourvel raises her eyes to his.

Tourvel Yes.

She collapses to her knees and throws her arms round his legs.

For God's sake, you must leave me, if you don't want to kill me, you must help, it's killing me!

Valmont, somewhat taken aback at first by her intensity, collects himself and lifts her to her feet. For a moment they sway together in an ungainly embrace; then Valmont leads her over to the chaise-longue where he deposits her gently. He leans forward to loosen her bodice as she stares helplessly up at him. He pauses for a moment, looking down at her. She holds his gaze. Something passes between them; and this time it's Valmont who looks away, something almost like shame darkening his expression. Then, to her surprise, he breaks away and runs over to the door, shouting.

Valmont Adèle!

He leaves the room; and a moment later, his voice is heard.

(*Off.*) Fetch Madame. Madame de Tourvel has been taken ill.

He hurries back into the room and over to the chaise-longue. As he arrives there, Mme de Tourvel reaches a hand up towards him. He takes it between both of his. He looks perplexed. He stands in silence, thoughtful, massaging her hand in his. Presently, Mme de Rosemonde appears, shepherded by her Maid. She clucks anxiously and hurries over towards the chaise-longue. Valmont releases Mme de Tourvel's hand.

She seemed to be having difficulty breathing.

Rosemonde Oh, my dear, whatever is it?

Mme de Tourvel stirs, managing a faint smile.

Tourvel It's all right, I'm all right now.

Valmont I shall leave her in your capable hands, Aunt. Send Adèle for me if I can be of any further assistance.

And, still looking strangely abashed, he leaves the room.

Rosemonde We must send for a doctor, my dear.

Mme de Tourvel is roused from her rapt contemplation of Valmont's departure.

Tourvel No, no, please, I don't need a doctor, I'm perfectly all right now.

Rosemonde We mustn't take any chances.

Tourvel No, I just . . . I must talk to you for a moment.

Mme de Rosemonde frowns, but without surprise. She turns to gesture at the Maid. The Maid curtsies and leaves. Mme de Tourvel motions Mme de Rosemonde to approach.

Come and sit by me. I can't speak very loud. What I have to say is too difficult.

I have to leave this house first thing in the morning. I'm most desperately in love.

To leave here is the last thing in the world I want to do: but I'd rather die than have to live with the guilt.

Rosemonde My dear girl. None of this is any surprise to me. The only thing which might surprise one is how little the world changes. Of course you must leave if you feel it's the right thing to do.

Tourvel And what should I do then? What's your advice?

Rosemonde If I remember rightly, in such matters all advice is useless. You can't speak to the patient in the grip of a fever. We must talk again when you're closer to recovery.

Tourvel I've never been so unhappy.

Rosemonde I'm sorry to say this: but those who are most worthy of love are never made happy by it. You're too young to have understood that.

Tourvel But why, why should that be?

Rosemonde Do you still think men love the way we do? No. Men enjoy the happiness they feel; we can only enjoy the happiness we give. They're not capable of devoting themselves exclusively to one person. So to hope to be made happy by love is a certain cause of grief. I'm devoted to my nephew, but what is true of most men is doubly so of him.

Tourvel And yet . . . he could have . . . just now. I saw his decision not to take advantage of me.

Rosemonde If he has released you, my dear child, it's because your example over these last few weeks has genuinely affected and improved him. If he's let you go, you must go.

Tourvel I will. I will.

Mme de Rosemonde sits, looking down, stroking Mme de Tourvel's hair, as the lights fade to black.

Act Two

ELEVEN

Mid-October. Valmont's bedroom in Mme de Rosemonde's château. Cécile is in bed with Valmont, taking dictation from him, pressing on his back, writing a letter to Danceny, who is seen, to one side, reading the letter.

As she writes, lights come up on the other side of the stage, revealing Mme de Merteuil, sitting at home, also reading the letter, with every evidence of enjoyment.

Cécile 'My dear Danceny . . .'

Valmont 'I swear to you . . .

Cécile writes.

. . . on my chastity, that, even if my mother forces me to go through with this marriage,' comma . . .

Cécile Comma . . .

Valmont 'I shall be yours completely.'

Danceny 'I shall be yours completely.'

Merteuil 'I shall be yours completely.'

Cécile continues to write; then she looks down at him, smiling roguishly.

Cécile 'Your good friend, the Vicomte de Valmont, has been exceptionally active on your behalf. I doubt if you could do more yourself.'

Merteuil laughs.
Cécile finishes writing. Valmont, amused, turns his head to kiss her.

Valmont You're outrageous.

Cécile Poor Danceny!

Valmont Nonsense, he'll be absolutely thrilled to get your letter.

Cécile All the same, I can't help feeling sorry for him.

Valmont No need for that. Remember our friend the Marquise de Merteuil's first rule in life?

Cécile No, what is it?

Valmont Never show pity. Especially to the vulnerable.

Cécile thinks about this for a minute.

Cécile Never show pity. Especially to the vulnerable.

TWELVE

Late October. The principal salon in le Vicomte de Valmont's Paris hôtel. Valmont sits at his desk, writing. He signs with a flourish and looks up as Azolan appears in the doorway and hurries into the room, pausing only to bow deeply.

Valmont Well, what treasures do you have in store for me today?

Azolan hands him two letters, one sealed and one unsealed.

Azolan A letter to Madame your aunt, sir. And this one, which Julie managed to get to before it was sealed up, to Madame de Tourvel's confessor.

Valmont Ah, very good!

He runs an eye quickly over the contents of the letter, then proceeds to seal it and his own letter as he speaks.

This is excellent, I have a letter for Father Anselme myself; you may deliver them both when you leave.

Azolan Yes, sir.

He takes the letters from Valmont.

Valmont And what news?

Azolan No visitors: there still hasn't been a single visitor
since she got back from the country. Kept to her room.
Bit of soup last night, but didn't touch the pheasant.
Afterwards a cup of tea. Nothing else to report. See, I was
right, wasn't I, sir, there was no need for me to join her
staff, now was there? I can find out everything you want to
know, no trouble at all.

Valmont I just thought you might prefer to be paid two
salaries. As at the time of the Duchesse.

Azolan Oh, well, sir, with Madame the Duchesse, that was
quite different, I didn't mind that at all. But I couldn't wear
a magistrate's livery, could I, sir, now be fair, not after being
in your service.

*He indicates his magnificent chasseur's uniform. Valmont
smiles, shaking his head. Then he opens a drawer and
hands him a small bag of money.*

Thank you, sir, thank you very much. One day I'll start
saving a bit, like you recommended, but I do like to do
justice to you.

Valmont After letting Madame de Tourvel leave my aunt's
house without even managing to warn me, you're lucky to
be working for anybody.

Azolan Now we've been through all that, sir, haven't we?
Not even Julie knew she was going till she went.

Valmont How is Julie?

Azolan Seems a bit keener than she was in the country.

Valmont And yourself?

Azolan shakes his head gloomily.

Azolan Talk about devotion to duty.

Valmont smiles and looks up as a Footman shows Mme de Merteuil and Danceny into the room. He rises to greet them, dismissing Azolan as he does so, speaking out of the corner of his mouth.

Valmont Off you go. Keep it up.

Azolan bows and leaves, together with the Footman.

Madame. My dear boy.

Danceny embraces Valmont impulsively.

Danceny Thank you, Monsieur, for everything.

Valmont holds him for a moment, smiling wickedly at Merteuil over Danceny's shoulder.

Valmont I was afraid I'd been a sad disappointment to you.

Danceny Of course I'm disappointed not to have seen Cécile for more than a month, but I believe I have you to thank for keeping our love alive.

Valmont Oh, as to love, she thinks of little else.

Danceny Anyway, how is she? That's what I've really come round to ask you, Monsieur.

Valmont Blooming. I really think the country air has done her good, I think she's even begun to fill out a little.

Danceny Really?

Valmont And of course she sends you all her love. She and her mother will be returning to Paris in about a fortnight.

Danceny I don't know how I can bear to go another two weeks without seeing her.

Merteuil We shall have to do our very best to provide some distraction for you.

Danceny Without your friendship and encouragement, I can't think what would have become of me.

Merteuil My dear, if you'd be so kind as to wait in the carriage for a few minutes, there's a matter I must discuss with the Vicomte in private.

Danceny Of course.

He bows to Valmont and pumps his hand heartily.

I don't know how I can ever repay you.

Valmont Don't give it another thought, it's been delightful.

Danceny smiles charmingly at them both and leaves the room. As soon as he's gone, Valmont and Merteuil burst out laughing and fall into each other's arms. They embrace for a moment and then pull apart, still smiling.

Poor boy. He's quite harmless.

Merteuil Well, I must say, I found Cécile's letter unusually witty.

Valmont So I should hope: I dictated it.

Merteuil Ah, Vicomte, I do adore you.

Valmont I have a piece of news I hope you might find entertaining: I have reason to believe the next head of the house of Gercourt might be a Valmont.

Merteuil What do you mean?

Valmont Cécile is two weeks late.

Merteuil is startled by this: she frowns, assessing its implications.

Aren't you pleased?

Merteuil I'm not sure. You have rather overstepped your brief.

Valmont Providing they hold the wedding before the end of the year, I don't see what harm can come of it.

Merteuil It just makes everything a good deal more chancy.

Valmont Your aim was to revenge yourself on Gercourt: I've provided him with a wife trained by me to perform quite naturally services you would hesitate to request from a professional. And very likely pregnant as well. What more do you want?

Merteuil All right, Vicomte, I agree, you've more than done your duty. Shame you let the other one slip through your fingers. I can only assume that's what happened?

Valmont's expression darkens.

Valmont I let her go. Can you imagine? I took pity on her. She was ready, the die was cast and the bill was paid. And I relented. And, what do you know, she vanished, like a thief in the night.

Merteuil Why did you let her escape?

Valmont I was . . . moved.

Merteuil Oh, well, then, no wonder you bungled it.

Valmont I had no idea she was capable of being so devious.

Merteuil Poor woman, what else could you expect? To surrender and not be taken, it would try the patience of a saint.

Valmont It won't happen again.

Merteuil What you mean is, you won't get the chance again.

Valmont Oh, yes, this time I have a foolproof plan.

Merteuil What, another one?

Valmont Absolutely guaranteed. I have an appointment to visit her at her house on Thursday. And this time, I shall be merciless. I'm going to punish her.

Merteuil I'm pleased to hear it.

Valmont Why do you suppose we only feel compelled to chase the ones who run away?

Merteuil Immaturity?

Valmont I shan't have a moment's peace until it's over, you know. I love her, I hate her, I'm furious with her, my life's a misery; I've got to have her so that I can pass all these feelings on to her and be rid of them.

Merteuil is beginning to look displeased. There's a pause, during which Valmont notices this and does his best to break the mood.

Now tell me what's happening in your life.

Silence. Merteuil considers.

Merteuil I'm not sure I care to just at the moment.

Valmont Oh, well, in that case, I shall have to conceal from you the details of my foolproof plan.

Merteuil That seems an acceptable enough bargain.

Valmont frowns, puzzled.

Valmont What's the matter?

Merteuil Nothing. I think I may have kept our young friend waiting long enough.

Valmont I shall call on you some time soon after Thursday.

Merteuil Only if you succeed, Vicomte. I'm not sure I could face another catalogue of incompetence.

Valmont Oh, I shall succeed.

Merteuil I hope so. Once upon a time you were a man to be reckoned with.

He makes to embrace her, but she limits herself to delivering a frosty peck on the cheek and hurries away. Valmont watches her go, troubled.

THIRTEEN

Six o'clock in the evening, a couple of days later. The salon in Mme de Tourvel's house, furnished in sombre good taste. Mme de Tourvel sits in an armchair, staring blankly at a piece of embroidery. On the other side of the room is an ottoman. Presently, Valmont is shown in by Father Anselme; as they appear, Mme de Tourvel makes an effort to stand, but is obliged to sit down again almost immediately. She's trembling. Father Anselme waits for a moment and is surprised to be dismissed with a gesture from Mme de Tourvel. Valmont, meanwhile, has bowed deep and now crosses the room to hand Mme de Tourvel a packet of letters, which she takes from him apprehensively.

Valmont I understand Father Anselme has explained to you the reasons for my visit.

Tourvel Yes. He said you wished to be reconciled with me before beginning instruction with him.

Valmont That's right.

Tourvel But I see no need for formal reconciliation, Monsieur.

Valmont No? When I have, as you said, insulted you; and when you have treated me with unqualified contempt.

Tourvel Contempt? What do you mean?

Valmont You run away from my aunt's house in the middle of the night; you refuse to answer or even receive my letters: and all this after I had shown a restraint of which I think we are both aware. I would call that, at the very least, contempt.

Tourvel I'm sure you understand me better than you pretend, Monsieur; it seemed to me by far the most . . .

Valmont Forgive me, I didn't come here to trade reproaches. You know your virtue has made as deep an impression on my soul as has your beauty on my heart. I suppose I imagined that made me worthy of you. What has happened is probably a just punishment for my presumption.

Silence.

My life has had no value since you refused to make it beautiful: all I wanted from this meeting, Madame, was your forgiveness for the wrongs you think I've done you, so I can at least end my days in some peace of mind.

Tourvel But you won't understand, I couldn't do what you wanted, my duty wouldn't allow me to . . .

Her voice tails off. Valmont moves a little closer and begins again.

Valmont It was me you ran away from, wasn't it?

Tourvel I had to leave.

Valmont And do you have to keep away from me?

Tourvel I do.

Valmont For ever?

Tourvel I must.

Silence. Then Valmont changes tack again, moving away this time.

Valmont Well. I think you'll find your wish that we be separated will succeed beyond your wildest dreams.

Tourvel Your decision is . . .

Valmont It's a function of my despair. I'm as unhappy as you could ever have wanted me to be.

Tourvel I've only ever wanted your happiness.

Valmont How can I be happy without you?

Silence. Mme de Tourvel is plainly distraught. Valmont appears to make a great effort to calm himself.

I'm sorry. I wanted to live for your happiness and I destroyed it. Now I want to give you back your peace of mind and I destroy that too. I'm not used to passion, I can't deal with it. At least, this is the last time. So be calm.

Tourvel It's difficult when you are in this state, Monsieur.

Valmont Yes; well, don't worry, it won't last very long.

He picks up the packet of letters, which Mme de Tourvel has let drop by her chair.

These are the only things which might weaken my courage: these deceitful pledges of your friendship. They were all that reconciled me to life.

He puts them down on the chair. Mme de Tourvel moves towards him, concerned.

Tourvel I understood you wanted to return them to me. And that you now approved of the choice my duty has compelled me to make.

Valmont Yes. And your choice has determined mine.

Tourvel Which is what?

Valmont The only choice capable of putting an end to my suffering.

Tourvel What do you mean?

Her voice is full of fear. Valmont is beside her now and she doesn't resist as he takes her in his arms.

Valmont Listen. I love you. You've no idea how much. Remember I've made far more difficult sacrifices than the one I'm about to make. Now goodbye.

He pulls away from her, but she clutches at his wrist.

Tourvel No.

Valmont Let me go.

Tourvel You must listen to me!

Valmont I have to go.

Tourvel No!

She collapses into his arms. He begins to kiss her and she responds: for a moment, they kiss each other greedily. Finally, he speaks with unusual tenderness.

Valmont Why should you be so upset by the idea of making me happy?

She looks up at him.

Tourvel Yes. You're right. I can't live either unless I make you happy. So I promise. No more refusals and no more regrets.

She kisses him.

FOURTEEN

The following evening. Mme de Merteuil's salon. She looks up as Valmont bursts ebulliently into the room, outpacing the Majordomo.

Valmont Success!

Merteuil At last.

Valmont But worth waiting for.

Merteuil flashes a chilly look at him, but he's too exhilarated to notice.

Merteuil So it worked, your foolproof plan?

Valmont Of course it wasn't foolproof, I was exaggerating to cheer myself up, but I did prepare the ground as carefully as I could. And I must say, considering these last few weeks my letters were all returned unopened, or rather my letter, since I simply placed it every other day in a fresh envelope, the result has been a genuine triumph.

By this time he's taken a seat and he pauses, beaming complacently at Merteuil.

Merteuil And the plan?

Valmont I began corresponding with Father Anselme, her confessor, an amiably dim-witted Cistercian, letting slip that I was losing the will to live, knowing that this would be passed on. I more or less forced him to arrange the meeting with her, in return for the privilege of being allowed to save my soul, a privilege he will now, poor man, be obliged to forgo. So, the threat of suicide, the promise of reform.

Merteuil I'm afraid I can't say I find that very original.

Valmont Effective though.

Merteuil Tell me about it.

Valmont Well, I arrived about six . . .

Merteuil Yes, I think you may omit the details of the seduction, they're never very enlivening: just describe the event itself.

Valmont It was . . . unprecedented.

Merteuil Really?

Valmont It had a kind of charm I don't think I've ever experienced before. Once she'd surrendered, she behaved with perfect candour. Total mutual delirium: which for the first time ever with me outlasted the pleasure itself. She was astonishing. So much so that I ended by falling on my knees and pledging her eternal love. And do you know, at the time, and for several hours afterwards, I actually meant it!

Merteuil I see.

Valmont It's extraordinary, isn't it?

Merteuil Is it? It sounds to me perfectly commonplace.

Valmont No, no, I assure you. But of course the best thing about it is that I am now in a position to be able to claim my reward.

Silence. Merteuil considers him coldly for a moment.

Merteuil You mean to say you persuaded her to write you a letter as well, in the course of this awesome encounter?

Valmont No. I didn't necessarily think you were going to be a stickler for formalities.

Merteuil Do you know, Vicomte, even if you had arrived with a letter up your sleeve, I'm not sure I wouldn't have had to declare our arrangement null and void?

Valmont What do you mean?

Merteuil I'm not accustomed to being taken for granted.

Valmont But there's no question of that, my dear. You mustn't misunderstand me. What in another case might be taken for presumption, between us, can surely be accepted as a sign of our friendship and confidence in each other. Can't it?

Merteuil I've no wish to tear you away from the arms of someone so astonishing.

Valmont We've always been frank with one another.

Merteuil And, as a matter of fact, I have also taken a new lover, who, at the moment, is proving more than satisfactory.

Valmont Oh? And who is that?

Merteuil I am not in the mood for confidences this evening. Don't let me keep you.

Silence. For a moment, Valmont is at a loss. Then he decides to persevere.

Valmont You can't seriously imagine there's a woman in the world I could ever prefer to you?

Merteuil I'm sure you're quite willing to accept me as an addition to your harem.

Valmont No, no, you've misinterpreted. What you think is vanity, taking you for granted: it's really only eagerness.

Merteuil's expression softens slightly, for the first time. Valmont is quick to sense this and immediately tries to press home his advantage.

I'd sacrifice anything or anybody to you, you know that.

Merteuil All right, Vicomte, let's try to discuss this calmly, shall we, like friends?

Valmont By all means.

Merteuil There's a strange thing about pleasure, haven't you noticed? It's the only thing that brings the sexes together; and yet it's not sufficient in itself to form the basis of a relationship. You see, unless there's some element of love involved, pleasure must lead directly to disgust.

Valmont I'm not sure I agree with that.

Merteuil Now, fortunately, it's only necessary for this love to exist on one side. The partner who feels it is naturally the happier; while the partner who doesn't is to some extent compensated by the pleasures of deceit.

Valmont I don't think I see your point.

Merteuil My point, Vicomte, is that you and I can in no way conform to this essential pattern, and we may as well admit it. Card sharps sit at separate tables.

Valmont Yes, and then they compare notes.

Merteuil Maybe: but without, I think, dealing a new hand.

Valmont I can't entirely accept the analogy.

Merteuil Don't worry: I shan't go back on our agreement. I have to go away for a couple of weeks . . .

Valmont What for?

Merteuil A private matter.

Valmont There was a time you kept no secrets from me.

Merteuil Don't you want me to finish what I was saying?

Valmont Of course, I'm sorry.

Merteuil When I've returned, and on receipt of this famous letter, you and I will spend a single night together. I'm sure we shall find it quite sufficient. We shall enjoy it enough to regret that it's to be our last; but then we shall remember that regret is an essential component of happiness. And part the best of friends.

Valmont I think we should take it one step at a time, don't you?

Merteuil No. I think we should be under no illusions.

Valmont You see, I don't think I've ever been unfaithful to you.

Merteuil You know, Vicomte, instead of trying to work on me in this, let's be frank, mechanical fashion, you should be thanking me.

Valmont What for?

Merteuil My courage. My stout resistance. My clear-sightedness. I understand, you see, what's going on.

Valmont Well, that's more than I can claim.

Merteuil I know. You may genuinely be unaware of this. But I can see quite plainly that you're in love with this woman.

Valmont No. You're wrong. Not at all.

Merteuil Have you forgotten what it's like to make a woman happy; and to be made happy yourself?

Valmont I . . . Of course not.

Merteuil We loved each other once, didn't we? I think it was love. And you made me very happy.

Valmont And I could again. We just untied the knot, it was never broken. It was nothing but a temporary . . . failure of the imagination.

Merteuil No, no. There would have to be sacrifices you couldn't make and I wouldn't deserve.

Valmont But I told you: any sacrifice you ask.

Merteuil Illusions, of course, are by their nature sweet.

Valmont I have no illusions. I lost them on my travels. Now I want to come home. As for this present infatuation, it won't last. But, for the moment, it's beyond my control.

Silence. She looks at him for a moment, considering.

Merteuil You'll be the first to know when I return.

Valmont Make it soon. I want it to be very soon.

He kisses her. She seems on the point of submitting to a long kiss, but then she breaks away abruptly and speaks with her usual control.

Merteuil Goodbye.

Valmont bows and hurries from the room. Merteuil stands a moment, collecting herself, then she crosses the room and opens a door.

He's gone.

Presently, Danceny steps into the room. He embraces her impulsively and, once again, she submits only briefly.

Danceny I thought he'd be here all night. Time has no logic when I'm not with you: an hour is like a century.

Merteuil We shall get on a good deal better if you make a concerted effort not to sound like the latest novel.

Danceny blushes.

Danceny I'm sorry, I . . .

Merteuil softens and reaches a hand to his cheek.

Merteuil Never mind. Take me upstairs.

Arm in arm, they begin to move towards the door.

FIFTEEN

*Valmont and Émilie, clasped in a tight embrace, dance
alone in a dimly lit ballroom. Gradually, the light rises and
more couples start joining them on the dance floor – among
them Cécile de Volanges and, eventually, Mme de Tourvel.
It doesn't take long for Tourvel to notice Valmont, who is
lost in another world with Émilie. Tourvel stops dancing,
watching them in growing horror. Suddenly, Valmont
becomes aware of Tourvel; immediately he breaks away from
Émilie and begins to move towards Tourvel: but she, blindly
bumping into the other dancers, stumbles out of the room.*

*As Valmont goes to follow her, he is intercepted by
Cécile, who is clearly in a state of some distress. He tries to
shake her off, but she clings to him and mutters urgently in
his ear, bent over in pain. He leads her to a side room. Once
there, she manages to loosen her skirt and remove it; her
petticoat is stained with blood. Cécile is terrified.*

Cécile What's . . . what's happening to me?

Valmont is thinking fast, assessing the situation.

Valmont You . . . I'm sorry to say . . . it looks very much as
if you're losing your baby.

Cécile Baby? What baby?

Valmont is taken aback; Cécile is processing what he's said.

You said . . . You told me that couldn't happen!

Valmont My dear, you mustn't believe everything you hear.

Cécile But . . .

*Valmont puts her back into her skirt; now, he grips her
under the arms.*

Valmont Come, hold on to me, keep your eyes down. I'm
going to take you to a surgeon.

He steers her out of the room and across the dance floor.

SIXTEEN

Mme de Tourvel's house. Tourvel, furious, sits writing a letter to Valmont – which he holds in his hand, reading it as he hurries across the stage.

Tourvel '. . . I feel sure you will no longer expect to be received in this house, Monsieur; and I feel equally sure that you will no longer wish to return here . . .'

She sits up at the sound of some commotion outside; and almost at once, Valmont bursts into the room, accompanied by Julie, Mme de Tourvel's maid, expostulating helplessly.

Julie I'm sorry, Madame, he . . .

Tourvel All right; leave us.

Julie leaves, flustered, still apologising. Tourvel speaks without looking at Valmont.

Obviously, you can't have read my letter.

Valmont But I have, Madame; over and over.

Tourvel Did I not make it clear that you would never be received here again?

Valmont You did.

Tourvel Then . . . ?

Valmont I felt it necessary to apologise to you in person. Otherwise I should never be able to forgive myself.

Tourvel looks at him for the first time; but says nothing.

Please allow me to explain.

Tourvel That woman you were with: I know her.

Valmont Are you sure? I'd be surprised.

Tourvel She's been pointed out to me at the Opéra.

Valmont Ah, well, yes, she is striking.

Tourvel She's a courtesan.

Silence.

Isn't she?

Valmont I suppose, in a manner of speaking . . .

Tourvel You may leave now.

Valmont sighs.

Valmont Unfortunately, I cannot unlive the years I lived before I met you; and, as I've explained, I had a wide acquaintance, the majority of whom were no doubt undesirable in one respect or another. Émilie, in fact, it may surprise you to learn, is one of the more intelligent and kind-hearted of my former friends; so when I ran into her again, I . . .

Tourvel I don't want to hear the sordid details.

Valmont Very well; but surely you're able to make a distinction between succumbing to an impulsive moment of self-forgetfulness – which led immediately, by the way, to shame and regret – and seeking to preserve the pure feelings of love and happiness that you and I have discovered together.

Tourvel Feelings which you have transformed into an insulting contempt. I don't know what I can have done to deserve it, this urge to humiliate me.

Valmont Humiliate you? How could I do that when I respect you as much as I love you? I know I'm guilty, I've admitted it. But I refuse to admit that this trivial lapse can be regarded as a crime against love.

Tourvel Evidently we have a different understanding of love.

Valmont Do we? That's not my recollection.

Silence. Mme de Tourvel looks at him, wavering.

Tourvel I do want to believe you.

Valmont Do you know what's really extraordinary about you?

Tourvel What?

Valmont You're completely incapable of disguising your feelings. I don't believe I've ever come across such a thing in a woman.

She looks up at him.

Tourvel Don't imagine that flattery can win you back my trust.

Valmont Of course, you have a perfect right to condemn me to eternal suffering. That would be no worse, I assure you, than this crippling sense I have of no longer deserving you.

Tourvel You're asking me to forget what happened?

Valmont Please, I beg you. It was the thoughtless behaviour of a man who had never met you.

He kisses her hand.

I didn't think it was possible for me to love you more.

He seems genuinely moved. Mme de Tourvel puts her arms around him.

Tourvel I love you so much.

He holds her; his expression is profoundly contented and uncharacteristically tender.

SEVENTEEN

Ten days later. Evening. Mme de Merteuil's salon.
A domestic tableau. Danceny lies on the sofa with his head
in Merteuil's lap. She plays idly with his hair.

To one side, isolated in a pool of light, is Cécile de
Volanges, evidently fully recovered. She's writing a letter; we
hear her voice.

Cécile 'My dearest Danceny, where are you? For a week
now, since Maman is away, I have been expecting your visit,
but nothing; silence.'

> *Unseen by Merteuil and Danceny and unaccompanied*
> *by servants, Valmont has been, for some time, standing*
> *in the doorway, watching. Now, he steps forward,*
> *clearing his throat, causing Danceny to shoot upwards in*
> *confusion. Merteuil looks up at him, her eyes cold.*

Valmont Your porter appears to be under the impression
that you are still out of town.

Merteuil I have in fact only just returned.

Valmont Without attracting the attention of your
porter? I think it may be time to review your domestic
arrangements.

Merteuil I'm exhausted from the journey. Naturally
I instructed my porter to inform casual callers that I was out.

> *Valmont seems to check a retort at this point, and turns*
> *instead, smiling, to Danceny.*

Valmont And you here, as well, my dear young friend.
The porter would appear to be having a somewhat erratic
evening.

Danceny Oh, well, I, erm, yes.

Valmont I'm glad to find you, I've been trying to contact
you for some days.

Danceny Have you?

Valmont Mademoiselle Cécile returns to Paris after an absence of over two months. What do you suppose is uppermost in her mind? Answer, of course, the longed-for reunion with her beloved Chevalier.

Merteuil Vicomte, this is no time to make mischief.

Valmont Nothing could be further from my mind, Madame.

Danceny Go on.

Valmont Imagine her distress and alarm when her loved one is apparently nowhere to be found. I've had to do more improvising than an Italian actor.

Danceny But how is she? Is she all right?

Valmont Oh, yes. Well, no, to be quite frank with you. I'm sorry to tell you she's been ill.

Danceny springs to his feet, horrified.

Danceny Ill!

Valmont Whether it was brought on by her anxieties it's impossible to say, but it seems about a week ago they were compelled to send for the surgeon in the middle of the night, and for a while he was very concerned.

Danceny But this is terrible!

Valmont Calm yourself, my friend, she has been declared well on the road to recovery. But you can well imagine how desperate I've been to find you.

Danceny Of course. My God, how could I have not been here at such a time? How can I ever forgive myself?

Valmont chooses not to answer this: he looks at Merteuil for a moment, assessing the damage.

Valmont But look, I hate to be the bearer of bad tidings.

He produces a piece of paper from an inside pocket.

It's just that I had a letter, the contents of which I thought might be of interest to the Marquise.

Silence. The ball is in Merteuil's court and she makes the effort to reach a decision.

Merteuil I think perhaps I should spend a few minutes with the Vicomte on a private matter. Why don't you go upstairs? I shan't be long.

Danceny But I'm worried about Cécile.

Merteuil I don't think there's anything to be done at this hour of the evening. You can send to enquire after her tomorrow.

Danceny Well, all right, if you say so.

Merteuil I do.

Danceny I'm sorry, Vicomte, I . . .

Valmont Don't upset yourself, dear boy, everything is as it should be.

Danceny Thank you. Thank you.

He leaves the room. Silence. Merteuil is about to speak, when Valmont interrupts her by handing her the letter. Merteuil gives it a cursory glance and then hands it back to Valmont.

Merteuil I see she writes as badly as she dresses.

Valmont I think I'm right in saying that in this case it's the content not the style which is the essential. But perhaps there's something else we should discuss first.

Merteuil I do hope you're not going to be difficult about Danceny: it was a complete coincidence he arrived at the gates at the same moment as my carriage.

Valmont Really, my love, this is hardly worthy of you. Given the uncharacteristic mystery you made about the identity of your new lover and Danceny's and your simultaneous disappearance from Paris, I would have to have been a good deal stupider even than you seem to assume I am, not to have reached the obvious conclusion. If Danceny and your carriage arrived at the gates at the same moment, I imagine the main reason was because he was in it.

Merteuil You're quite right, of course.

Valmont And furthermore, I happen to know that this moment of which we speak occurred two days ago.

Merteuil Your spies are efficient.

Valmont So much for my being the first to know when you returned. A lesser man might allow himself to get angry.

Merteuil Such a man might risk losing his ability to charm, without necessarily enhancing his power to persuade.

Silence. Valmont restrains himself and decides to change tack.

Valmont I must say I'm not surprised you chose to be reticent about so manifestly unsuitable a lover.

Merteuil My motive had nothing whatever to do with his suitability.

Valmont I mean, I know Belleroche was pretty limp, but I think you could have found a livelier replacement than that mawkish schoolboy.

Merteuil Mawkish or not, he's completely devoted to me, and, I suspect, better equipped to provide me with happiness and pleasure than you in your present mood.

Valmont I see.

Slightly winded by this, he lapses into an injured silence. Merteuil's mood, however, now she has regained the initiative, seems to have improved.

Merteuil So is it really true the little one has been ill?

Valmont Not so much an illness, more a refurbishment.

Merteuil What can you mean?

Valmont At the Comtesse de Beaulieu's ball, a couple of weeks ago, she suddenly began to display some unmistakable symptoms. After that, it was a real test of ingenuity, getting her to the surgeon, without giving ourselves away.

Merteuil But you evidently succeeded?

Valmont Can you imagine, my dear, it turned out Cécile wasn't even aware of being pregnant in the first place. She certainly doesn't devote any undue energy to thinking.

Merteuil Well, Vicomte, I'm sorry about the loss of your son and Gercourt's heir.

Valmont Oh, I thought you'd be pleased, you seemed notably disgruntled about it when I first told you.

Merteuil Once I got used to the idea, I began to enjoy it. I think you should make another attempt, don't you?

Valmont I rather felt the moment had come to pass her on to young Danceny.

Silence. Merteuil considers for a moment.

Merteuil No, I'm not sure that would be advisable just now.

Valmont Oh, you don't?

Silence.

Merteuil If I thought you would be your old charming self, I might invite you to visit me one evening next week.

Valmont Really.

Merteuil I still love you, you see, in spite of all your faults and my complaints.

Valmont I'm touched. What else will you exact before honouring your obligations?

There's a pause, during which Merteuil looks mischievously at Valmont.

Merteuil I have a friend, who became involved, as sometimes happens, with an entirely unsuitable woman. Whenever any of us pointed this out to him, he invariably made the same feeble reply: 'It's beyond my control,' he would say. He was on the verge of becoming a laughing stock. At which point, another friend of mine, a woman, decided to speak to him seriously, and, most importantly, drew his attention to this linguistic foible, of which he'd previously been unaware, and told him his name was in danger of becoming ludicrously associated with this phrase for the rest of his life. So do you know what he did?

Valmont I feel sure you're about to tell me.

Merteuil He went round to see his mistress and bluntly announced he was leaving her. As you might expect, she protested vociferously. But to everything she said, to every objection she made, he simply replied: 'It's beyond my control.'

Long silence. Eventually, Valmont rises.

Valmont I must leave you to your lessons.

Merteuil doesn't answer. She watches him, smiling, as he moves, deep in thought, towards the door.

EIGHTEEN

*The following afternoon. The salon in Mme de Tourvel's
house. As her Footman shows in Valmont, she springs to
her feet, unable to conceal her delight. He, however, looks
strained and weary; and advances almost reluctantly into the
room, as the Footman leaves them. Mme de Tourvel runs
over to him and buries herself in his arms. He embraces her
almost involuntarily, bracing himself against what is to come.*

Tourvel You're only five minutes late, but I get so frightened.
I become convinced I'm never going to see you again.

*Valmont carefully disentangles himself and puts some
distance between them before he speaks.*

Valmont My angel.

Tourvel Is it like that for you?

Valmont Oh, yes. At the moment, for example, I'm quite
convinced I'm never going to see you again.

Silence. Tourvel frowns, trying to make sense of this.

Tourvel What?

Valmont I'm so bored, you see. It's beyond my control.

Tourvel What do you mean?

Valmont After all, it's been four months. So, what I say. It's
beyond my control.

Tourvel Do you mean . . . do you mean you don't love me
any more?

Valmont My love had great difficulty outlasting your
virtue. It's beyond my control.

Tourvel It's that woman, isn't it?

Valmont You're quite right, I have been deceiving you with
Émilie. Among others. It's beyond my control.

Tourvel Why are you doing this?

Valmont Perhaps your merciless vulnerability has driven me to it. Anyway, it's beyond my control.

Tourvel I can't believe this is happening.

Valmont There's a woman. Not Émilie, another woman. A woman I adore. And I'm afraid she's insisting I give you up. It's beyond my control.

Suddenly, Mme de Tourvel rushes at him, fists flailing. They grapple silently and grimly for a moment, before she screams at him.

Tourvel Liar!

Valmont You're right, I am a liar. It's like your fidelity, a fact of life, no more nor less irritating. Certainly, it's beyond my control.

Tourvel Stop it, don't keep saying that!

Valmont Sorry. It's beyond my control.

Mme de Tourvel screams.

Why don't you take another lover?

She bursts into tears, shaking her head and moaning incoherently.

Just as you like, of course. It's beyond my control.

Tourvel Do you want to kill me?

Valmont strides over to her, takes her by the hair and jerks her head up, shocking her into a moment's silence.

Valmont Listen. Listen to me. You've given me great pleasure. But I just can't bring myself to regret leaving you. It's the way of the world. Quite beyond my control.

When he lets go of her hair, she collapses full-length, moaning and sobbing helplessly. Valmont crosses to the

*doorway and turns to look back at her. His triumphant
expression has lasted only a moment; and now gives way
to a queasy, haunted, tormented look. His eyes are full
of fear and regret. For a moment, it's almost as if he's
going to run back to help her; but, abruptly, he turns and
guiltily scuttles away.*

NINETEEN

*About a week later. A December evening in Mme de
Merteuil's salon. Merteuil sits at a small escritoire, writing.
After a time, Valmont appears in the doorway, once again
unannounced. Merteuil, with her back to the door, doesn't
see him, but as he approaches, she looks up, hearing a
footstep, and speaks without turning round.*

Merteuil Is that you? You're early.

Valmont Am I?

*Merteuil spins around, startled; to be greeted with an
ironic bow from Valmont.*

I wanted to ask you: that story you told me, how did it end?

Merteuil I'm not sure I know what you mean.

Valmont Well, once this friend of yours had taken the
advice of his lady friend, did she take him back?

Merteuil Am I to understand . . . ?

Valmont The day after our last meeting, I broke with
Madame de Tourvel. On the grounds that it was beyond my
control.

*A slow smile of great satisfaction spreads across
Merteuil's face.*

Merteuil You didn't!

Valmont I certainly did.

Merteuil Seriously?

Valmont On my honour.

Merteuil But how wonderful of you. I never thought you'd do it.

Valmont It seemed pointless to delay.

Merteuil With the anticipated results?

Valmont She was prostrate when I left. I called back the following day.

Merteuil You went back?

Valmont Yes, but she declined to receive me.

Merteuil You don't say.

Valmont Subsequent enquiries I made established that she had withdrawn to a convent.

Merteuil Indeed.

Valmont And she's still there. A very fitting conclusion, really. It's as if she'd been widowed.

He reflects for a moment, then turns to her, radiating confidence.

You kept telling me my reputation was in danger, but I think this may well turn out to be my most famous exploit. I believe it sets a new standard. I think I could confidently offer it as a challenge to any potential rival for my position. Only one thing could possibly bring me greater glory.

Merteuil What's that?

Valmont To win her back.

Merteuil You think you could?

Valmont I don't see why not.

Merteuil I'll tell you why not: because when one woman strikes at the heart of another, she seldom misses; and the wound is invariably fatal.

Valmont Is that so?

Merteuil I'm so convinced it's so, I'm prepared to offer any odds you care to suggest against your success.

Some of the self-satisfaction has ebbed out of Valmont's expression.

You see, I'm also inclined to see this as one of my greatest triumphs.

Valmont There's nothing a woman enjoys as much as a victory over another woman.

Merteuil Except, you see, Vicomte, my victory wasn't over her.

Valmont Of course it was, what do you mean?

Merteuil It was over you.

Long silence. The fear returns to Valmont's eyes. He begins to look cornered. Merteuil, on the other hand, has never seemed more serene.

That's what's so amusing. That's what's so genuinely delicious.

Valmont You don't know what you're talking about.

Merteuil You loved that woman, Vicomte. What's more, you still do. Quite desperately. If you hadn't been so ashamed of it, how could you possibly have treated her so viciously? You couldn't bear even the vague possibility of being laughed at. And this has proved something I've always suspected. That vanity and happiness are incompatible.

Valmont is very shaken. He's forced to make a great effort before he can resume, his voice a touch ragged with strain.

Valmont Whatever may or may not be the truth of these philosophical speculations, the fact is it's now your turn to make a sacrifice.

Merteuil Is that right?

Valmont Danceny must go.

Merteuil Where?

Valmont I've been more than patient about this little whim of yours, but enough is enough and I really must insist you call a halt to it.

Silence.

Merteuil One of the reasons I never remarried, despite a quite bewildering range of offers, was the determination never again to be ordered around. I decided if I felt like telling a lie, I'd rather do it for fun than because I had no alternative. So I must ask you to adopt a less marital tone of voice.

Valmont She's ill, you know. I've made her ill. For your sake. So the least you can do is get rid of that colourless youth.

Merteuil I should have thought you'd have had enough of bullying women for the time being.

Valmont's face hardens.

Valmont Right. I see I shall have to make myself very plain. I've come to spend the night. I shall not take at all kindly to being turned away.

Merteuil briefly consults the clock on her desk.

Merteuil I am sorry. I'm afraid I've made other arrangements.

A grim satisfaction begins to enliven Valmont's features.

Valmont Ah. I knew there was something. Something I had to tell you. What with one thing and another, it had slipped my mind.

Merteuil What?

Valmont Danceny isn't coming. Not tonight.

Merteuil What do you mean? How do you know?

Valmont I know because I've arranged for him to spend the night with Cécile.

He smiles charmingly at her.

Now I come to think of it, he did mention he was expected here. But when I put it to him that he really would have to make a choice, I must say he didn't hesitate for a second. He knew his mind.

Merteuil And now I know yours.

Valmont He's coming to see you tomorrow to explain and to offer you, do I have this right, yes, I think I do, his eternal friendship. As you said, he's completely devoted to you.

Merteuil That's enough, Vicomte.

Valmont You're absolutely right. Shall we go up?

Merteuil Shall we what?

Valmont Go up. Unless you prefer this, if memory serves, rather purgatorial sofa.

Merteuil I believe it's time you were going.

Silence.

Valmont No. I don't think so. We made an arrangement. I really don't think I can allow myself to be taken advantage of a moment longer.

Merteuil Remember I'm better at this than you are.

Valmont Perhaps. But it's always the best swimmers who drown. Now. Yes or no? Up to you, of course. I wouldn't dream of trying to influence you. I therefore confine myself to remarking that a 'no' will be regarded as a declaration of war. So. One single word is all that's required.

Merteuil All right.

She looks at him evenly for a moment, almost long enough for him to conclude that she has made her answer. But she hasn't. It follows now, calm and authoritative.

War.

Blackout.

TWENTY

The stage is divided into four separate areas: in the centre, is a clearing in the Bois de Vincennes at dawn, where Danceny, accompanied by his second, paces up and down impatiently, épée in hand; elsewhere, Mme de Merteuil sits at her escritoire, writing; Valmont is also in the process of writing a letter; and Mme de Tourvel lies in a curtained bed in the convent, critically ill, attended by a surgeon and Mme de Volanges.

Merteuil 'My dear Chevalier Danceny, I understand you spent last night with Cécile Volanges.'

Danceny has paused to consult the letter. Mme de Merteuil breaks off, thinking.

Valmont 'My dear aunt, in the event the day does not go well for me, I have asked my man Azolan to pass on to you this letter: which contains my last (and most urgent) request.'

Mme de Rosemonde is reading this letter.

Merteuil 'I learned of this, you may be interested to hear, from her more regular lover, the Vicomte de Valmont.'

The light snaps out on Merteuil.

Valmont 'I want you to go and see Madame de Tourvel in the convent, where I'm told she lies gravely ill, and give her a message from me.

104

I want you to tell her that I can't explain why I broke with
her as I did, but that since then, my life has been worth
nothing.

The duel begins, scrappy and brutal.

Tell her it's lucky for her that I'm gone and I'm glad not to
have to live without her. Tell her her love was the only real
happiness I've ever known.'

*Tourvel cries out again; and again it's as if Valmont hears
her. He seems to come to a decision and deliberately
turns onto Danceny's blade, which penetrates his body,
just below the heart. He crashes to the ground. Danceny
immediately drops to one knee beside him.*

Danceny Fetch a surgeon!

Valmont No, no.

Danceny Do as I say!

*Azolan and Danceny's second run off, leaving Danceny
alone with Valmont. Valmont gestures feebly at Danceny.*

Valmont A moment of your time.

*Danceny gently lifts him into a sitting position. Valmont,
with some difficulty, fetches out of his coat pocket a
bloodstained package of letters.*

These are from the Marquise de Merteuil.

Danceny I . . .

Valmont Read them. You will see quite clearly that in this
affair, we are both her creatures.

He hands the letters to Danceny, who, overcome with emotion, puts up a hand to brush away a tear.

Don't feel badly, my young friend: you had good cause. I don't believe that's something anyone's ever been able to say about me.

He raises a hand towards Danceny, but slumps back before Danceny can take it. He's dead.
Mme de Rosemonde, accompanied by Mme de Volanges, has arrived at the convent and been shown into Mme de Tourvel's room. She leans forward to murmur into Tourvel's ear. She speaks for some time; then Tourvel raises a hand.

Tourvel Enough!

TWENTY-ONE

In the background, the Comtesse de Beaulieu's ball is taking place in her grand salon. Merteuil approaches; she seems subdued, under some kind of a strain. She encounters Cécile, who, on the contrary, looks serenely at ease. It's night. The two ladies exchange salutations.

Cécile Are you quite well, Madame?

Merteuil I am. Naturally, I was distressed to hear that our dear friend, Madame de Tourvel, had passed away.

Cécile Yes, my mother told me it was one of the most terrible deaths you can possibly imagine.

Merteuil Really? In what way?

Cécile They tried everything: cupping her and bleeding her; but she kept ripping away the bandages and reopening the wounds. Delirium. Convulsions. And she wouldn't eat; in the end she just wasted away.

Merteuil I see.

Cécile She said to my mother, over and over again: 'I'm dying because I wouldn't believe you.'

Merteuil Believe her about what?

Cécile The warnings my mother tried to give her about Valmont.

Merteuil Ah, Valmont . . .

She breaks off, clearly affected, though she tries to conceal this by changing the subject.

Strange thing happened just now, when I arrived: this woman, I can never remember her name, but she's always perfectly pleasant. Anyway, I greeted her in the usual way and she turned her back on me.

Cécile appears to hesitate for a moment before speaking.

Cécile I think I might be able to explain.

Merteuil Explain? What can you explain?

Cécile I understand that, just before he died, the Vicomte de Valmont was able to hand over to Danceny a bundle of letters.

The blood drains from Merteuil's face; but she recovers quickly.

Merteuil And . . . ?

Cécile I think . . . copies of those letters may have been circulated.

Merteuil But hasn't Danceny run away to Malta?

Cécile It appears he may have passed the letters on to someone else.

Merteuil But who? Who could he possibly . . . ?

She breaks off. Cécile says nothing. Slowly, it dawns on Merteuil what must have happened.

Why on earth would you want to do such a thing?

Cécile doesn't answer.

You must surely have known that making those letters public would ruin my good name for ever. And, among them, are a number of letters that will do the same for you.

Cécile Yes, those letters I took the precaution of destroying.

Merteuil shakes her head, baffled.

Merteuil But . . . why have you done this?

Cécile takes her time before answering.

Cécile When you were advising me – a course of instruction for which I will be eternally grateful – you told me nothing could strengthen a woman's reputation for virtue more than to denounce the sins of others.

Merteuil is staggered.

I'm sure, under the circumstances, you'll understand that I can no longer invite you to be my Matron of Honour. As the Comtesse de Gercourt, I really can't afford to take any risks.

Merteuil shakes her head, even more astonished.

Merteuil I thought we were friends.

Cécile Oh, we are. We always will be. But I was following your first rule in life.

Merteuil Which is?

Cécile Never show pity. Especially to the vulnerable.

Merteuil Who told you that?

Cécile He did.

She slips away; and, gradually, Merteuil is surrounded by people passing letters to one another, jostling her, involving her in a kind of poisoned dance; finally, engulfing her altogether – and then, eventually, spitting her out, jeering at her, their movements ever more hostile.

Then they're gone: and Merteuil is alone, weary, fragile, frightened. The darkness swallows her up.